THE ENDURING
PORTLA
BLACK
PANTHERS

THE ROOTS OF
FREE HEALTHCARE,
FREE BREAKFAST,
AND NEIGHBORHOOD
CONTROL IN OREGON

JOE BIEL
FOREWORD BY AARON DIXON

MICROCOSM PUBLISHING
PORTLAND, ORE AND CLEVELAND, OH

THE ENDURING LEGACY OF PORTLAND'S BLACK PANTHERS
THE ROOTS OF FREE HEALTHCARE, FREE BREAKFAST, AND NEIGHBORHOOD
CONTROL IN OREGON

© Microcosm Publishing, 2023

ISBN 9781648411816
This is Microcosm #703
First Published November, 2022
This edition © Microcosm Publishing, 2022

All author proceeds are being donated to the movement
Cover illustration by Gerta O Egy.

For a catalog, write or visit:
Microcosm Publishing
2752 N Williams Ave.
Portland, OR 97227
www.Microcosm.Pub/BlackPanthers

To join the ranks of high-class stores that feature Microcosm titles, talk to your rep: In
the U.S. **Como** (Atlantic), **Abraham** (Midwest), **Book Travelers West** (Pacific), **Turnaround**
in Europe, **Manda/UTP** in Canada, **New South** in Australia, and **GPS** in Asia, India, Africa,
and South America. We are sold in the gift market by **Faire.**

Library of Congress Cataloging-in-Publication Data

Names: Biel, Joe, author.
Title: The enduring legacy of Portland's Black Panthers : the roots of free
    healthcare, free breakfast, and neighborhood control in Oregon / by Joe
    Biel.
Description: [Portland] : Microcosm Publishing, [2022] | Summary: "In the
    1960s through 1980s, the Black Panther Party rose up throughout the
    United States, envisioning a world without systemic racism and police
    violence. This is the story of Portland, Oregon's chapter of the Party,
    told from original interviews, first-hand accounts, and extensive
    research, including police surveillance documents. This account shows a
    vivid picture of neighborhood activists determined to improve their
    community by creating their own social services, and wildly
    succeeding-despite the best attempts of police, city officials, and
    media to paint them as violent extremists, and to spy on, infiltrate,
    and violently suppress their activities. Portland's Black Panther
    chapter innovated healthy free breakfasts for children in poverty, the
    longest-running Panther free health clinic, and a powerful system of
    self-directing neighborhood
    associations. Joe Biel's account shows that the Portland chapter's
    successes resound to this day, with current programs for free breakfasts
    in schools, Portland's strong neighborhood association systems, and even
    the Oregon Health Plan owing their existence to Black Panther
    initiatives. Despite a racist city hall and police force, Black Panthers
    in Portland persisted, outlasting most branches in the United States and
    permanently changing the city for the better."-- Provided by publisher.
Identifiers: LCCN 2022014733 | ISBN 9781648411816 (trade paperback)
Subjects: LCSH: Portland Black Panthers--History. | African
    Americans--Oregon--Portland--History--20th century. | African
    Americans--Oregon--Portland--Social conditions--20th century. | Portland
    (Or.)--Race relations--History. | Portland (Or.)--Politics and
    government--20th century. | African Americans--Politics and
    government--Oregon--Portland.
Classification: LCC F884.P89 B53 2022 | DDC
    322.4/20979549--dc23/eng/20220331
LC record available at https://lccn.loc.gov/2022014733

MICROCOSM·PUBLISHING

Microcosm Publishing is Portland's most diversified publishing house and distributor with a focus on the colorful, authentic, and empowering. Our books and zines have put your power in your hands since 1996, equipping readers to make positive changes in their lives and in the world around them. Microcosm emphasizes skill-building, showing hidden histories, and fostering creativity through challenging conventional publishing wisdom with books and bookettes about DIY skills, food, bicycling, gender, self-care, and social justice. What was once a distro and record label started by Joe Biel in a drafty bedroom was determined to be *Publisher's Weekly's* fastest growing publisher of 2022 and has become among the oldest independent publishing houses in Portland, OR and Cleveland, OH. We are a politically moderate, centrist publisher in a world that has inched to the right for the past 80 years.

Did you know that you can buy our books directly from us at sliding scale rates? Support a small, independent publisher and pay less than Amazon's price at **www.Microcosm.Pub**

Global labor conditions are bad, and our roots in industrial Cleveland in the 70s and 80s made us appreciate the need to treat workers right. Therefore, our books are MADE IN THE USA

TABLE OF CONTENTS

SUPP-ORT
A MUNI
TRO
PoLic
GN
HE PETI

Police Surveillance Photo, February 14, 1970, Courtesy of Portland City Archives A2004-005.2958 : Black Panthers demonstration in support of "repressed peoples." U.S Courthouse.

ACKNOWLEDGEMENTS

Without the work of the following people, there is no way that I could have finished this book.

- Dominic Nigro, who worked on this book with me from 2004–2010, gave me the confidence and gumption to believe that this was a project that I was capable of completing and answered questions over the past few years when I decided to finish it.

- Floyd Cruse was supportive of this project from the beginning and offered his knowledge and network as a Black Panther.

- Alec Dunn wrote the first accounts that I saw of Portland's Black Panthers in the zine *Nosedive* in 1997. When I sent him some fan mail and let him know about this project, he was nice enough to direct me to the few books that reference the Portland chapter. His work taught me that even as a punk kid without a formal education, I could write about complex subjects.

- In the final stages, Adam Carpinelli provided vital services of interpreting between Kent Ford and the publisher to ensure that this book was of the highest quality possible.

- Jane Cigarran provided vital support and feedback at the last minute, both in terms of fascinating details and corrections.

- Dylan Ray for securing photography reproduction rights.

- Jules Boykoff and Martha Gies created immensely important groundwork and provided thoughtful feedback.

- Kent Ford trusted me with his story and spent many hours on the phone with me as he remembered stories and details. The more I get to know him, the more I find him inspiring and wise.

- The work of Dr. Judson L. Jeffries, Lucas N. N. Burke, and David Walker were instrumental to making this book possible. The hours they spent researching and reporting on these subjects made this project hundreds of hours of work instead of thousands. Additionally, the feedback and encouragement from Burke and Dr. Jeffries were helpful in finally wrapping this up.

- Intisar Abioto offered me solid encouragement and support about the importance of this documentary work and the importance of the Panthers' legacy.

- Andrea Washington and Jamaal Green found value in this project and appreciated my efforts to approach it sensitively, offering to help bridge my experiences as a white person.

- Sarah Koch, my editor, always asked the difficult questions in the simplest language, two things I truly appreciate.

- Percy Hampton, who took my first phone call, even without an introduction, and relayed his story and experiences honestly and thoughtfully, despite many similar interviews over fifty years.

- Sandra Ford and Jon Moscow were instrumental for confirming many suspicions that I had and rumors relayed to me. Their commitments to activism past retirement age will always be an inspiration.

- Esa Grigsby managed the final text massaging and caught a number of factual bits, contested across various sources.

- Chantal James provided insightful editing, compliments, encouragement, and sensitivity reading regarding my blind spots as a white person embarking upon this project.

- Aaron Dixon for being yet another inspiration in life and in offering the foreword for this book.

- Elly Blue has supported my reporting passions for fifteen years, even interrupting quality time so I could take unscheduled phone calls from Kent Ford for this book. Elly always encouraged me to pursue my passion for this project.

Street scene in Albina neighborhood, 1966, courtesy of Portland Archive

FOREWORD

*D*uring the turbulent and rebellious years of the 1960s, it seemed that America was beginning a new age of awakening and a desire for more of a true sense of freedom. From the Deep South to the East and West Coasts, the rebellious youth of America revolted against the old order in a bid to expose the old lies of history so that a new reality could emerge for shaping a better future for this country.

Many of the stories of these intense struggles taking place throughout America would make it into the headlines. In 1965 the Watts riots erupted into national attention soon to be followed by rebellions throughout the land. New York, Harlem, New Jersey, Boston, Chicago, and many other larger and smaller communities throughout the land would find themselves pulled into the melee.

But there were quiet, quaint communities that we heard little about, and one of those small places was Portland, Oregon. *The Enduring Legacy of Portland's Black Panthers* gives us a glimpse into how far reaching this time was even in small town America.

This book also sheds light on the history of Portland, Oregon—now considered the whitest city in America—and the founding of the Portland chapter of the Black Panther Party and their struggle to bring justice for blacks and others in this small Northwest city. We learn of one of the founders of this small, obscure chapter, Kent Ford, who would lead the Portland chapter through victories and defeats. And we see the difficulty of organizing in isolation from Black urban centers on the West Coast.

This isolation played a key role in the Portland chapter developing into a Panther chapter that had a uniqueness about it. Most Panther chapters were a microcosm of their surroundings and history, and we see that played out in this history. We hear about the development of the city's first free medical and dental clinic, and the treachery that Kent Ford and his comrades were continuously faced with as they attempted to establish their enduring legacy.

This book is a must read for anyone who thinks they are students of the 60s and the history of the Black Panther Party.

—Aaron Dixon
Former Captain of the Seattle chapter of the Black Panther Party

INTRODUCTION

*W*henever I bring up the Black Panther Party for Self-Defense, people bristle. The Black Panthers are primarily remembered for standing up to the violence of the state and for their iconic photos in leather jackets and berets, brandishing rifles like they were willing to use them. Due to the racist history of how Black people have been viewed and treated in the United States—as well as how information about the Panthers has been filtered and distorted by the state—people tend to believe the narrative that the Panthers were a terrorist organization trying to overthrow the U.S. government. But this is far from the truth.

And in Portland, Oregon, the Black Panthers almost exclusively focused on developing social programs. They monitored the police but didn't engage in armed standoffs or shoot-outs. They mostly fed, clothed, educated, and healed the poor—Black and white alike. In return, the public was deceived through misinformation while the Panthers were singled out and targeted by the FBI. On a walking tour of the Albina neighborhood in 2022, a white woman who had lived nearby in the 1970s shared that—based on everything she had heard at the time—she was afraid of the Party when it was active. Convinced that their fellow members were working for the FBI, the Panthers were violently dismantled by the government throughout the '70s and '80s. Like most of history, the victors took the spoils and told the story that they wanted. So, the legacy of the Panthers is attributed to everyone besides the people who did the work.

In the late '90s, I heard a lot about the Portland Panthers but—as a white person—I was outside of communities who had documentation or a complete narrative, there were just bits and pieces strewn about. People told me that the Panthers were responsible for the Oregon Health Plan and the dental clinic on Flint Avenue that I passed on my way downtown. I had long heard rumblings and rumors about free meals, scuffles with the police, and how it all tied to one of the first single-payer healthcare systems in the U.S. It felt like a puzzle to untangle the truth.

So in 2004, Dominic Nigro and I began work on a book about the Portland Black Panthers. He was acquainted with a number of the surviving members so we began making phone calls. We dug through microfiche at the downtown public library. We scheduled interviews, and former Panther Floyd Cruse—deputy minister of information for the Portland chapter—started hanging around Microcosm's office inside Liberty Hall on N Ivy Street, telling stories. Cruse's job had been to give speeches on behalf of the Party and he still loved that role. Each tidbit and discovery felt like a needle in a haystack. Dominic and I tried to piece a story together. We felt tremendous immediacy in this work. One by one, the members were dying off and there was still very little documentation of their accomplishments or even their organization—despite its many positive changes and impacts on the city of Portland.

Almost immediately, we were crashing into roadblocks. The Portland Panthers had been disbanded—like many local Black Panther Party chapters—through a series of FBI Counterintelligence Program (COINTELPRO) campaigns to confuse and divide the group into distrusting their collaborators. Just about every former member refused to participate in interviews if we included another core member of the group, that, 45 years later, they were still convinced was an FBI informant. Worse, some of them *were* working with the FBI. But which ones? Sowing this confusion and distrust was a core tactic of the FBI in the '60s so it was heartbreaking to see how effective it had been. Dominic decided that he could no longer participate if each person's participation meant the exclusion of another member. To him, this meant that we should cancel the project in 2010. To me, these were still captivating personalities drenched in controversial and dramatic idealism. They had been more successful than anyone else I'd ever met. While their story lacks the episodic nature of *Star Wars* and is thoroughly unsuited for Hollywood, if you pull back the frame, the thematic stakes and wider drama of the Portland Black Panthers are similar. They created unlikely coalitions of rebel armies to prevent the takeover of an all-powerful sinister empire, through exploiting secret weaknesses.

Of course, I have never been one to give up easily—if at all. When the definitive book *Black against Empire: The History and Politics of the Black Panther Party* was published in 2013, I cracked it open and, to my horror, I discovered that it didn't contain a single reference to the existence of the chapter in Portland. This was so shocking that my intent on telling this story was renewed. And there were encouraging signs over the years. Sarah Mirk researched the history of Portland's Black Panthers and Know Your

City published her work as a comic in 2011. I contacted her, inquiring about the possibility of her expanding the work and she explained that she had run into the same problem, citing the difficulty of getting members to participate and lingering distrust among the surviving members. She expressed that a longer piece would be difficult. Know Your City dissolved as an organization in 2019 and took their publishing rights with them. They expressed interest in turning these rights over and I've followed up every three months about republishing these comics but, between the legal rules of how ending a nonprofit is handled and moving on with their lives, these stories may be lost to history.

Another beacon of hope appeared in 2016, when University of Washington Press published Lucas N. N. Burke and Dr. Judson L. Jeffries's *The Portland Black Panthers: Empowering Albina and Remaking a City*. After reading the book, I was shocked that in 250 pages it barely mentioned COINTELPRO and did not mention impediments to conducting the research. I contacted both authors to ask them if they had run into the same issues that Sarah, Dominic, and I had. Dr. Jeffries explained that infighting and distrust among surviving members was an issue he had faced in virtually every Black Panther chapter that he had interviewed and that he did not have any greater trouble navigating it in Portland. However, he said that fear of who was a COINTELPRO infiltrator did not pose a significant impediment to the research process. Has the situation changed? Was my whiteness posing a barrier? Regardless, Dr. Jeffries's thousands of hours of interviews created the first holistic framing of the organization that made it much easier to put the puzzle pieces together and made this book possible.

Over the past eighteen years, members of Portland's Black Panther Party have continued to pass away, including Floyd Cruse, who could no longer thumb through publications in Microcosm's office. Fortunately, Cruse can be remembered by the bootleg "best of" editions that he published of the *Black Panther* newspaper. His presence in the rapidly gentrifying Albina[1] neighborhood felt like some of the last vestiges of the '60s, long after the central neighborhood had been razed to the ground.

Indeed, sixty years later, Microcosm's office still overlooks dozens of empty lots that used to contain Portland's "Black downtown," but are now overfill parking for a hospital where people let their dogs poop and houseless people camp. In a city with a housing crisis and an utter lack of land to utilize, what series of events make sense to let millions of dollars worth of valuable property sit unused? What happened here?

I asked early Panther recruit Percy Hampton why he thought Party members were initially hesitant to talk to me and he turned the question on its head, "A lot of people weren't as actively involved in the Black Panthers as they thought they were. Before I retired, I was trying to hide from the persona so my boss didn't start asking questions while lots of other people were trying to take credit for the work that we did." This made more sense to me and I had seen this in all manner of activist organizing. But then who controls their legacy?

---

1 Now Boise-Eliot

I know that bureaucracy can destroy anything that is remotely interesting, but how much of what I'd heard was true? I had to find out. There are a lot more resources to draw from in 2022 than in 2004 and if the surviving members were talking, it finally felt like there was a clear path forward. So I decided to give former Black Panther captain Kent Ford a phone call out of the blue. It was a Sunday afternoon and he was attending a BBQ, but he answered anyway. It was hard to tell if he remembered me from my initial research or not. Now 78 years old, Ford didn't miss a beat. "Remind me about what you're doing. Let's get together next weekend."

It's clear that Ford gets phone calls like mine all the time. People want him to tell his story. Even in his late 70s, Ford still has the activist spirit and remains ready to fight for justice. He remains critical of people who give interviews in the press but don't show up to protests. He was enthusiastically still the same activist who stood on the justice center steps making speeches in 1969. And indeed, in 2020 when Portland had two hundred consecutive nights of daily racial justice protests, Ford was there every night as though fifty years had not passed. By this point, I had read a dozen books that made reference to the Portland Black Panthers and Ford's life and just needed to fill in some gaps.

Ford and I met in his old neighborhood, at NE 15th and Broadway. Kent is warm, magnetic. It feels good to be around him. He feels aware of how he's coming across, with an underlying intensity. He listens well and offers honest compliments.

Immediately, we are running into people that he has known for years. He pointed out former landmarks to me. I expected him to be weary and wary but he was enthusiastic and modest. He walked so fast that I had trouble keeping up. I received the earnest impression that he still genuinely enjoys community organizing. In 2020, he began giving six walking tours of the Black Panthers' history each year.

•   •   •

I asked Ford if he ever sought out his FBI file and he said that he doesn't want to know what's in there—and he believes that he has a pretty good idea already. He recalls a story about how in the '70s, a neighbor saw five strangers entering his house with a key. The contents of his home were tossed and when he asked his landlord how they could have obtained a key, he said that he provided one. He tells me another story about the police finding a car containing a .45 pistol. He recounts how the FBI sat him down and demanded that he sign an agreement admitting that the gun was his, but telling him that the document was just acknowledging their meeting. Suddenly looking concerned, Ford exclaims to me, "If I had signed that form, that would have been it. They would have put me away for who knows how long. They want everyone to get in line and I wasn't going to do that."

Over the course of a few hours seated upstairs at Lloyd Center mall, the conversation about the distant past is draining. Ford shared stories of being jailed without charges, of being framed for crimes, of having guns planted on him, of being told to sign papers that confessed to crimes, of having the FBI try to turn his friends against him—and some of them taking the bait. Just revisiting the events of Ford's life, I came home exhausted. There are so many heartbreaking and tragic moments and when you draw a line through that narrative, I'm unsure how anyone could carry on. Incidents like this in your life make you question who you can trust and Ford says that he's still processing a lot of them and putting together what happened, fifty to sixty years later. Ford has traveled down this road so many times. I am heartened by his willingness to do it once more.

I can understand why Kent Ford was reluctant to talk in the past and I'm glad for the opportunity. He asks me if I know the difference between authors James Baldwin and Ta-Nehisi Coates. "Yeah, Coates's audience is white," I quip. It catches him off guard. Ford begins to tell me his oft-repeated statement that Coates was not as involved in the struggle as Baldwin.[2] But Ford interrupts himself, "Yes, that's true also." He pauses to reflect for a moment. "But authors like that serve an important role too," I continue. He nods. At this moment, as a white person, it feels like I may have won Ford's trust. Nearly every day from that point forward, he gives me a call to recount another story or detail that he remembers and suggests more leads to investigate. Ford gave me contacts for surviving members, suggested which newspapers were in league with the FBI, recalls getting beat up by cops in the McDonald's parking lot, and told me story fragments about the corrupt history of Mayor Terry Schrunk's administration or how even Black leaders like Charles Jordan had their hands tied by the city's power structure. I enjoy our talks and when

2 While this is true, James Baldwin was born in 1924 while Ta-Nehisi Coates was born in 1975, when the world and the struggle had significantly changed. Coates's father, W. Paul Coates, was the Maryland State Coordinator of the Black Panther Party and publisher of Black Classic Press.

I don't hear from Ford for 24 hours, I start to worry about him. I wonder how much our relationship is influencing my reporting, but his memory is remarkable. I fact-checked things thoroughly and investigated discrepancies with him. With this book, it's very satisfying to close this loop and untangle such an elaborate web.

You might read this book expecting that there will be extensive footnotes, accounts of episodes, and direct interviews. Often, I could not go into as much detail as I would have liked because sources were missing, important people had passed away, or I couldn't verify a single account against anything. In many cases, my whiteness likely created a barrier to people sharing stories with me and gaining access to their history. In most cases, I established trust over time, but in others, people passed away or their mental facilities had deteriorated due to age before we could speak on the record. While I talked—directly or indirectly—to all living Portland Black Panthers who were willing to speak to me, the situation was frequently fractured because of old rivalries or information lost to time.

Everything in this book was verified in personal interviews, against the newspaper accounts of these events, by comparing notes against accounts from available witnesses, and—most importantly—against the few books in print on these matters, chiefly *The Portland Black Panthers: Empowering Albina and Remaking a City*. Despite the growing volume of information and references available about the Portland Black Panther Party in 2022, virtually all of it still lives and dies in the intellectual ghetto of academia. When I asked people if they had read *The Portland Black Panthers*—

including people who work in academia—100 percent of people in my poll responded that they own it but had not read it. It was absolutely soul crushing that people still didn't know about this vital history. So that's why this is not an academic book, but a popular history. My original mission from 2004 is just as valid today as it was then—to tell the story of the Portland Black Panther Party's legacy in simple language, in a sequential narrative, in one place, and to boost the signal of an underreported chapter to the general population in a book that people will excitedly crack open and devour.

After eighteen years of digging, I decided that I would rather publish an imperfect book than lose so many of these details to history. I know that for each new book published on a topic, it opens a door for other authors to unearth new pieces of the past in future books. I've done my best to honor the fabric of stories that were shared with me about this delicate moment in history, though I may have missed details and some people may likely disagree about aspects of these events. If you have more perspectives or details, I'd love to hear from you and include greater depth in a future edition. I hope that there are many more books published about these groups and events from this period in Portland's history. Sometimes, even the past is unwritten—but the future certainly is.

A WHITE COLONY IN CRISIS

*B*efore we get into the story of the Black Panther Party itself, we need to look to history in order to understand why Portland's population remains over 70 percent non-Latino white and why the Portland Panthers were organizing. Even when massive 2020 Black Lives Matter protests made national news in Portland—the vast majority of participants were white. Or as Seyi Fasoranti, a Black chemist who moved to Oregon in 2020, told the *New York Times*, "There are more Black Lives Matter signs in Portland than Black people." It's an uncomfortable truth. Our brand of liberal values feels deeply invested in "proving" that we aren't racist—without performing a proper inventory and evaluation of the truth of that statement. Why do white people have such a near-monopoly on inherited wealth, business, homeownership, and culture in a neoliberal city that regards itself as politically progressive?

In 1837, Oregon created a state constitution that forbade Black people from residing in Oregon,[3] owning property, or being party to a contract. In short, Black people could not rent property, receive work, or functionally benefit in any way from Oregon. This law also affected cultural attitudes towards Black people. When Alonzo Tucker was shot and thrown off a bridge in 1837, no charges were filed against his murderers and the *Oregon Journal* referred to the mob who killed him as

---

3 Oregon's first black exclusion law stated that Black people attempting to settle in Oregon would be publicly whipped with 39 lashes every six months until they left Oregon.

"quiet and orderly." It almost felt like they were celebrating the murderers for having "good manners."

By 1900, Black people comprised merely 0.25 percent of Portland's population. As a result of laws, attitudes, segregation, sharecropping, thousands of lynchings,[4] and dehumanizing horrors in the South, millions of Black families moved west during the Great Migration of 1916. Most people headed for Los Angeles, Oakland, or Seattle, only to find different forms of oppression and a lack of opportunities. In 1919, hundreds of Black people were murdered by white mobs during "Red Summer," in forty different staged attacks across the United States. In 1921, the "Black Wall Street" of Greenwood in Tulsa, Oklahoma was completely destroyed when a Black man was accused of raping a white woman.[5] Two years later, the same thing happened in Rosewood, Florida.

In 1922 Oregon was the only West Coast state that allowed the Klu Klux Klan to intimidate its foes publicly and boasted 35,000 members. Portland was a leading center for KKK recruitment, in 1923 with the *Portland Telegram* reporting that the Portland Police Bureau was "full to the brink with Klansmen." The Klan held initiation ceremonies on Mt. Scott in Portland, the burning crosses visible for miles. The local KKK Grand Dragon worked with Portland Police to handpick one hundred Klansman to designate as legal vigilantes with badges. The KKK voted their biggest critic, Ben Olcott, from the governor's seat and replaced him with

4 These horrific events were heralded as public entertainment and accompanied with commemorative postcards. Anti-lynching legislation was not successfully passed until 2020.
5 For more on this, check out Kris Rose's *White Riot / Black Massacre: A Brief History of the 1921 Tulsa Race Massacre*

their own candidate. In the '20s, the only reason Black people were tolerated in Portland is because the locals hated Chinese and Japanese immigrants *more*. Employers treated Black people as a workforce they could underpay and overwork. Many Black people worked for the long-distance railroad and settled around the train station downtown. The 1837 law was enforced less and less. Still, in 1925, Lee Anderson, a Black Portlander, commented, "We are surrounded by a prejudice that you do not see in our neighboring states."

In Portland, as Black families shifted away from work as railroad porters to own businesses and work as hotel maids, they moved out of downtown and headed north. They settled into homes on the other side of the Willamette River, in Portland's first suburb, Albina, annexed by Portland in 1891. Even then it was mostly a small collection of farms, houses, and trees—named after the founder's daughter. Albina was the site of Oregon Railway & Navigation Company, which connected Portland to the East Coast, chosen solely for its cheap land and a newly constructed bridge connecting it to Portland.

In 1926, the clause excluding Black residents from Oregon was finally overturned by popular vote. Still, Black people were prohibited from owning homes elsewhere in Portland due to redlining practices, lending discrimination, contracts preventing homes from being sold to Black people, and forced segregation. As a result, Black families had no choice but to create Portland's first Black community, with 53 percent owning their homes in Albina. Nationally, Black voices shifted from pleading for freedom and equality to demanding the ability to accumulate economic power and inherited wealth—just like white people. Albina was the site of the first Black funeral home, which still exists today, alongside many other Black-owned businesses. The neighborhood was a reflection of the shifting attitudes of Black people in the United States and their ability to create the world they wanted to see.

However, white Americans were not ready for change. In retaliation for founding the Universal Negro Improvement Association—espousing views that Black people should have financial independence and be proud of their racial heritage—Marcus Garvey was deported to Jamaica in 1927. His views were ahead of his time and the tensions around how to significantly change attitudes towards Black people in the United States slowly escalated into a mounting culture war.

During World War II, massive shipbuilding efforts suddenly required a rapidly growing population in Portland. Sensing the opportunity, over three hundred Black residents from New York City moved to Portland for jobs building war vessels on Swan Island—a stone's throw from Albina. When these jobs were denied to Black people, conflict escalated. A one hundred thousand person march on Washington for Civil Rights was planned until President Roosevelt agreed to pass an executive order forbidding hiring discrimination for wartime jobs. The march was canceled and as a result, at least twenty thousand Black transient workers flocked to Portland for these industrial jobs. The white city government panicked, with one city councilman suggesting that so many Black migrants would require "a policeman on every corner." Instead, the city built Vanport, the United States's largest wartime public housing project. Vanport consisted of slum tenement homes capable of housing sixteen thousand migrant workers and was located on the Columbia River between Oregon and Washington—surrounded by industrial waste. Vanport was poorly built, poorly run, and widely segregated. About 12 percent of the original residents were Black. More even than Albina, Vanport hired Black residents for government jobs, including teachers and law enforcement. After the war, despite its initial temporary nature, the Vanport Housing Project continued to exist and grew to become 33 percent Black as white people returned to where they came from.

In 1945, Irving Jones, a Black man, was mistaken for someone with a warrant and shot by Portland Police through his own window. Officers were found not guilty for the shooting, even though they had murdered someone other than whom they intended and made no attempt to peacefully arrest him first. It's baffling how the court could arrive at this logic puzzle and ruling, even though it's unsurprising how it transpired. First, the ruling claims that it is okay for the Portland Police to murder people who pose no threat to them. Second, the ruling shows that it doesn't matter if police murder the wrong person because they can claim to have believed it was someone else. This loose logic slowly forms the foundation for the development of policing in Portland.

However, in 1948, Vanport was decimated by heavy rain, an early thaw, and a broken dike on the Columbia River. As the flood loomed, the 16,931 residents were advised not to evacuate. There was insufficient housing and food for Portland to put them elsewhere. Inevitably, the houses—which lacked foundations—were swept away as the floodplain filled. There are heartbreaking photos of well-dressed Black families attempting to carry what possessions they can lift over their heads as the flood comes up to their shoulders. While the official death toll is only thirteen, many residents believe that the vast majority of deaths went unreported. Equally grim, everything was destroyed and no compensation was given—setting back the residents of Vanport economically for decades. Today, Vanport is rebuilt as a raceway, golf course, and industrial park with no signs of the former toil. And you can rest assured that the dikes that protect that precious golf course are much better engineered.

Police began allowing national criminals to live in Portland—in return for a payoff. During prohibition, Portland Police controlled the supply—and thus price—of whiskey within the city. By the '40s, Portland Police managed a criminal racketeering, brothel, and gambling operation.[6] Police officers collected the equivalent of over half a million dollars in today's money in bribes and payoffs. The police's theory was that if there was going to be prostitution, gambling, and drugs in the city, wasn't it better to have it under government control? The police centralized many of their vice businesses in Albina, using the justification that *this is where all crime happens anyway*. Mayor Fred Peterson thought he was in charge of overseeing these businesses and gave permission to a friend to open a vice business. Immediately, the police busted it up—revealing to the mayor that the crime boss, James Elkins, was actually running things.

6 "Organizing Portland Organized Crime, Municipal Corruption, and the Teamsters Union." *History Cooperative*, 17 Feb. 2020, historycooperative. org/journal/organizing-portland-organized-crime-municipal-corruption-and-the-teamsters-union/.

The FBI installed a massive wiretapping operation in 1954 and found that Mayor Peterson and the police chief were working for and protecting criminal enterprises.[7] From 1956–1957, 115 Portland police officers were indicted for involvement in these crimes. The district attorney, mayor, and police chief were brought up on charges of working for Elkins. Just as it was about to go to trial, Bobby Kennedy brought them in to testify on national television in a federal trial against Jimmy Hoffa. But it was a trick. Elkins had planted a fake story that the teamsters were running the vice operation in Portland. Elkins was upset that the district attorney had begun working for his rival and decided to tear the whole thing down. When the dust settled, nobody was convicted. Reforms to the systems that made this criminal racketeering operation possible were minimal. Business mostly continued as usual.

7 *Portland Confidential: Sex, Crime, and Corruption in the Rose City,* Phil Stanford, 2018

Kent Ford, 2022, on walking tour in front of former site of dental clinic

A MOUNTING CULTURE CLASH

*I*n 1953 the Klan burned a cross on the lawn of a Black family that moved into Portland's Parkrose neighborhood—open housing legislation had finally put an end to redlining within city limits. In 1955, fourteen-year-old Emmett Till was visiting his uncle in Mississippi when he allegedly whistled at a white woman. In response, after three days of torture and mutilation, a gang of white people brutally murdered him and deposited his corpse in the Tallahatchie River. His mother insisted on transporting his body back to their home in Chicago for an open casket funeral so that the world could see what racism justified in the American consciousness. Photos of Till's disfigured corpse appeared in newspapers and magazines all over the United States.

That same year in Montgomery, Alabama, fifteen-year-old Claudette Colvin refused to give up her seat on the bus and was arrested. Nine months later, the incident was recreated with Rosa Parks refusing to give up her seat on the bus. While Colvin was a righteously angry teenager, Rosa Parks was the upstanding and respectable secretary of the local Montgomery National Association for the Advancement of Colored People (NAACP). Being a polite liberal in glasses with an impeccable record, it was difficult to paint Parks as a criminal. The NAACP recognized that they needed a character above reproach to recreate this event for the national news in order to demonstrate the injustices at work. The stunt was a success, and Black people launched a bus boycott in Montgomery, Alabama, forcing the courts to desegregate public transportation across the country.

The year prior, the Supreme Court ruled in *Brown v. Board of Education* that schools were separate but not equal and that they must be integrated. Nationally, violent clashes ensued as schools attempted to desegregate. Despite the Supreme Court ruling, in 1957 the governor of Arkansas refused to let nine Black students attend public high school in Little Rock, so the students were escorted to school by the U.S. Army amid violent threats. Many students had to be escorted to school by federal troops all over the country as most white people remained resistant to this cultural shift.

The desegregation of schools and transportation and the story of Emmett Till launched the U.S. civil rights movement. Voices like Dr. Martin Luther King Jr. and the Southern Christian Leadership Conference (SCLC) offered a new strategy—to put anger aside, arguing that any violence from Black people was counterproductive. They suggested that Black people should turn the other cheek instead of fighting back against their violent, white oppressors. Soon after this declaration, the 16th Street Baptist Church in Birmingham was bombed, killing four children. No charges were filed against anyone for over a decade. Public killings of dozens of Black leaders working for justice made many activists question this strategy. Clearly, white people and the state were not committed to nonviolence. Yet, in many ways, Dr. King was correct: the spectacle of Black people being brutalized was a powerful one. It not only created sympathy, but it showed the oppression of Black people to anyone who had not experienced similar oppression.

Back in Portland, under the leadership of Mayor Schrunk in 1958, the city created the Portland Development Commission (PDC) to "promote industrial expansion," without any limits on its powers. Once the PDC declared an area to be a "slum," they had rights to redevelop as they pleased.

By 1960, 73 percent of Portland's fifteen thousand Black residents lived in Albina and white residents' attitudes became increasingly polarized. In sixty years, the Black population of Portland had grown 2,143 percent to become 4 percent of the city. And yet, even in Albina, whites comprised 66 percent of the population in the "Black neighborhood."

One of the PDC's first projects was to declare central Albina to be in "an advanced stage of urban blight," explaining, "clearance appears to be the only solution . . . to avoid the spread of that blight to other surrounding areas." The PDC made sure to note that the real estate was useful and centrally located. It appeared that the City of Portland would again take away many Black people's homes and inherited wealth as history continued to repeat itself.

The PDC's plans set out to eliminate the homes of one-third of all Black Portland homeowners. The PDC applied for hundreds of millions in federal funds to redevelop Albina without community input, but the Black community organized and responded. A retired schoolteacher, Leo Warren, formed the Emanuel Displaced Persons Association (EDPA). She loved her neighborhood, offering tours to show that it was not blighted at all. She proclaimed, "In listening to people from all over Portland, we could get the idea that you were doing us all a favor; that all homes in the displacement area were bad, and that we should be grateful for your attention." Leo Warren and the EDPA fought back in the courts, claiming that the PDC was exhibiting discrimination of citizen participation in a federal program, due to the sources of funding. With support from the NAACP, the EDPA pushed back and the plan was restructured. As a compromise, the amount of destruction was lessened and the PDC agreed to buy every house in the neighborhood at a value reduced from its market rate.

Despite occasional concessions, no one knew just how much the U.S. government was willing to escalate its emboldened war on Black people. In 1915, after a mob had assassinated Haitian President Jean Vilbrun Guillaume Sam, the United States sent five thousand Marines to seize the country. The United States executed political dissidents,[8] enacted systems of forced labor, occupied Haiti for decades, caused thousands to die, leveraged Haitian land sales to U.S. companies, and made the small island nation a servant of Wall Street.[9] The Marines leveled machine guns into unarmed crowds, any Haitians carrying guns were shot on sight, and stories abound of public lynchings of dissidents.[10] President

8 "The long legacy of the U.S. occupation of Haiti." *The Washington Post*, 6 Aug. 2021, washingtonpost.com/history/2021/08/06/haiti-us-occupation-1915/

9 The U.S. State Department summarized thusly, "Between 1911 and 1915, seven presidents were assassinated or overthrown in Haiti, increasing U.S. policymakers' fear of foreign intervention. In 1914, the Wilson administration sent U.S. Marines into Haiti. They removed $500,000 from the Haitian National Bank in December of 1914 for safe-keeping in New York, thus giving the United States control of the bank."

10 Smedley Butler, a general for the U.S. Marine Corps later regretted these actions, saying "I spent thirty-three years and four months in active military service as a member of this country's most agile military force, the Marine Corps . . . During that period, I spent most of my time being a high-class muscleman for Big Business, for Wall Street, and for the Bankers. In short, I

Woodrow Wilson created the Haitian-American Treaty of 1915, giving the United States control of Haiti's finances and forcing the legislature to install a president favorable to U.S. interests. Even by U.S. imperialist standards, the invasion and occupation was devastatingly brutal and has destabilized the island nation into the present. However, Haiti would not be the last Black nation that the United States would seek to control.

In 1960, Patrice Lumumba was the first democratically elected leader of the Congo after the country achieved independence from Belgium. As a civil war brewed in his country, he asked the United States for help and was declined. When Lumumba asked the Soviet Union for help, CIA agent Larry Devlin sent a message back to headquarters, proclaiming, "Patrice Lumumba was born to be a revolutionary, but he doesn't have the qualities to exercise power once he's seized it. Sooner or later, Moscow will take the reins. He believes he can manipulate the Soviets, but they are the ones pulling the strings." His boss, Allen Dulles, responded, "If Lumumba continues to be in power, the result will be at best chaos and at worst an eventual seizure of power by the communists, with disastrous consequences for the prestige of the UN and the interests of the free world. His dismissal must therefore be an urgent and priority objective for you." So President Eisenhower and the CIA recruited Lumumba's political enemies and coordinated a death squad to violently dismember Lumumba's body and melt him in acid in 1961.[11]

was a racketeer, a gangster for capitalism."

11 "The C.I.A. and Lumumba." *The New York Times*, The New York Times, 2 Aug. 1981, nytimes.com/1981/08/02/magazine/the-cia-and-lumumba.html

It was perhaps a new low: the United States would overturn democratic elections in Africa and violently murder its leader when they couldn't control him. For reaching out to the Soviet Union, U.S. Secretary of State C. Douglas Dillon described Lumumba as an "irrational, almost psychotic personality." How would Dillon describe Eisenhower, Dulles, and Devlin for manufacturing a plot to murder a democratic leader simply because they could not control him? Regardless, it's a horrific war crime and bold terrorism. The Congo, a country rich with mineral resources, was establishing financial stability and independence for the first time, but this assassination and further power struggles between global powers have kept the country in a state of flux, fighting for legitimacy and stability to this day.

Back in the United States, the civil rights movement seemed to only create more racial and cultural tension across the country. In 1962, Dr. George Simkins Jr., a dentist in Greensboro, referred a Black patient to Moses H. Cone Memorial Hospital, a private white-owned facility. When the hospital refused the referral, the NAACP attempted to refer another Black patient to Greensboro's other private white hospital, Wesley Long, who also refused. Black doctors who attempted to work at either one were refused as well. Since both hospitals received federal funding, Simkins made the case for discrimination and in 1963, the *Simkins v. Cone* Supreme Court case found that Black people could no longer be discriminated against in healthcare. It was a ruling as important as *Brown v. Board of Education* was ten years earlier. Unfortunately, as many people have discovered, you cannot legislate respect, and tensions merely worsened.

Similar to the bus boycotts in Alabama, sit-ins were staged at whites-only lunch counters in Tennessee and North Carolina. Calm and peaceful Black college students would take a seat at the whites-only counter until they were arrested.[12] These students implemented the teachings of Dr. Martin Luther King Jr. with a confrontational edge—so that when violence was used against them, it would demonstrate their point and make white onlookers sympathetic to their oppression. Simultaneously, these actions showed how far whites would go to uphold segregation. And the rising tide of these conflicts was only getting bloodier.

In response to 41 Black leaders and 74 others being murdered for their work in the civil rights movement, Robert F. Williams created the Black Armed Guard of North Carolina. After a 1961 armed standoff in which the Guard traded bullets with the Klu Klux Klan, he fled to Cuba where he broadcast his *Radio Free Dixie* program to the South and wrote his book *Negroes with Guns*. Unconvinced by the doctrine of Dr. King, Williams felt that Black people had to be armed and on the defensive.

The dangers and risks were difficult to deny—even by Dr. King—who began to predict his own impending death. Armed defense security groups formed to provide protection for voter registration and so Black organizations could remain nonviolent. Others didn't eschew violence. Stokely Carmichael saw the weakness of nonviolence, pointing out that the Klu Klux Klan weren't afraid to use their guns and suggested that Black people shouldn't be either. In Lowndes County, Alabama, where the Democratic Party was still

12 For more on these protests and why they were so successful, check out *How to Boycott: Make Your Voice Heard, Understand History, & Change the World*

segregationist, Black people created their own party with Carmichael, using a pouncing black panther as their logo. The members carried guns as basic protection for pending attacks.

Malcolm X, founder of the Organization of Afro-American Unity, famously kept violence on the table as an option. He referred to himself as a "realist," pointing out that the only people asked to be nonviolent are Black people. Malcolm X was the son of a Baptist preacher, who believed in the teachings of Marcus Garvey. Malcolm's father was murdered by white extremists, which only drove his teachings home. Malcolm X became disillusioned with the teachings of the Nation of Islam and the sexual ethics of his mentor, Elijah Muhammad. He sought new methods to build a civil rights movement.

In 1963, when John F. Kennedy was murdered by a sniper in Dallas, it was a rallying cry for Civil Rights. Kennedy had been a major proponent for racial justice and this drove many theories about the motive for his murder. However, Malcolm X's comfort with embracing violence could not protect him either. While giving a talk in 1965, and in the presence of undercover agents, he was gunned down as his wife and daughters desperately tried to hide. The press had even received phone calls the morning of the assassination, informing them that Malcolm X would be murdered that day. Three members of the Nation of Islam were charged with the murder and spent nineteen years in prison until withheld FBI documents implicated other suspects and revealed that at least two of them were innocent. By the time that he was found innocent, one suspect had already passed away. The other was 83 years old at the time of the trial. Suspicions about who was actually responsible for the murders of John F. Kennedy and Malcolm X flared, and this 2021 trial only gave more ammunition to the people who had known this for 35 years. The greatest question remains, *if the police and FBI knew that Malcolm X was to be murdered and had undercover officers onsite, why didn't they stop the assassination?* We may never know who the three gunmen were who rushed the stage that night and these events only further damaged the ability of Black people in the United States to trust their own government.

Also in 1965, a Los Angeles police officer pulled over a man for drunk driving. The man resisted arrest, with help from his mother. In return, the man was beaten in the face with the cop's baton as a crowd of onlookers stared, horrified. Onlookers even claimed that the police had kicked a pregnant woman present in the crowd. The punishment did not fit the crime and for the next six days, the Watts Riots ensued, leaving 34 dead and $40 million in damage, only ending with the arrival of fourteen thousand National Guardsmen. The prevailing feeling was that Black people had no route to justice or equal treatment under the law. When James Meredith, a lone Civil Rights marcher in Memphis, was shot by a sniper, many activists questioned King's views on nonviolence even further, including Stokely Carmichael.

Yet in 1966, 86 percent of Portland police officers still believed that the civil rights movement was happening "too fast." Because of attitudes like this, in the summer of 1967, Black uprisings exploded in ten cities, including Portland. A peaceful march ended in violence, with rocks and bottles thrown at white passersby near Irving Park, resulting in four hundred officers being dispatched, who shot one man and arrested 98 more. But the wreckage was vast: angry residents had torched city equipment, destroyed fuel trucks, broke windows, and looted nearby businesses. When Kent Ford was asked his opinion on looting by professor Jules Boykoff in 2020, he responded, "The United States has been looting Black communities forever." Ford's thoughts resonate similarly to remarks from heavyweight boxer Muhammad Ali in 1966, who explained that he was being asked to murder Brown people in Vietnam, another poor country, only to come home to Louisville, where Black people were treated like dogs.

In response to these national uprisings, the federal government issued the Kerner Report in 1968, saying that this Black violence was caused by social ostracism, lack of employment options, lack of education options, and racial segregation. They correctly pointed out that by resolving these four key issues, the problem would be solved. But Portland wasn't ready to listen. In 1968, Kenneth Gervais's study of the Portland Police Bureau found that officers believed that surveillance of Black people was justified. A group of teenagers in Portland attempted to have a meeting with Mayor Schrunk, requesting three hundred jobs, better education, and the withdrawal of the police from Irving Park. The mayor declined all three requests. Black voices turned up by the hundreds to demand a voice in how the Portland Development Commission was going to redevelop *their* neighborhood. In 1967, a young Black man commented to the newspaper, "Where else but Albina do cops hang around streets and parks all day like plantation overseers?" This conflict began showing up on the radar of the federal government. The U.S. Department of Housing and Urban

Development office hesitated giving funds to Portland, insisting that the PDC hadn't sought community involvement in the redevelopment of Albina.

Two months after the Kerner Report, Dr. Martin Luther King Jr. was assassinated in Memphis after being pressured by the FBI into a hotel room where he was susceptible to attack. Freedom of Information Act (FOIA) files showed that FBI Director J. Edgar Hoover had lost his temper when Dr. King spoke against the war in Vietnam. The FBI responded by painting Dr. King as a communist,[13] bribing his friends to betray him, sending undercover operatives to disrupt his peaceful protests, manufacturing the appearance of multiple sexual affairs, and sending him repeated letters urging him to kill himself. FOIA files released in 2001 show that military snipers were stationed on nearby roofs and CIA agents were deployed to the scene. James Earl Ray, who was arrested for the murder, was never allowed to receive a trial and died in prison. A 1999 federal civil trial led by Coretta Scott King and Dexter King found that agencies of the United States government had been partially responsible for his murder,[14] confirming what Black people have long feared and suspected.

Then, in 1972, another suspicion was confirmed: it was revealed that Black people were the unwitting subject

13 This is false. Dr. King believed that communism allowed evil and destruction just like capitalism, couched in moral justification and relativism. He felt that communism was a contradiction of his devout Baptist beliefs of God providing for our needs. Being referred to as a communist was suggesting that Dr. King was under the influence of foreign governments during the Cold War and is similar to referring to someone as a terrorist today.

14 *An Act of State: The Execution of Martin Luther King*, William Pepper, Verso Press, 2018 and you can read more in *The CIA Makes Science Fiction Unexciting: Dark Deeds & Derring-Do*

of harmful medical experiments. Since 1932, the U.S. Public Health Service promised free medical care to six hundred Black men in Tuskegee, Alabama. Many had never before visited a doctor. Instead of care, two-thirds of the subjects had been selected because they had syphilis. The doctors wanted to study how the disease progressed unhindered. When penicillin became the standard treatment for syphilis, the men were instead given mineral supplements and aspirin. The conspiracy extended to local doctors who agreed not to treat the men. Even as the men began to go blind, lose mental facilities, have severe health problems, and die—no penicillin was given to them. A researcher was horrified to learn about this study, and when a committee of his white superiors did not find any ethical concerns, he brought the story to the press. The doctors had planned to continue the study until all participants died but public outcry ended the Tuskegee Syphilis Experiment in 1972, but not before the disease had been spread to children and loved ones.

Even 75 years after the Civil War Reconstruction era, the combination of physical, mental, emotional, and economic violence targeting Black Americans continually demonstrated the need for a movement that advocated, educated, and practiced self-defense against a slowly encroaching series of horrors. And a few college students in Oakland had some new ideas about what that could look like.

A PARTY FOR SELF-DEFENSE

*I*n 1967, the Portland Police responded to a burglary in Kent Ford's Albina apartment. Due to now-public records we have learned that—despite being the victim of a crime—instead of helping him, the police used the break-in as an opportunity to file a police report on Ford as a "possible subversive." Ford's crimes? He was reading Mao and decorated his walls with maps of Vietnam and Cambodia. Ford claims that $1,000 was missing. The police never recovered the stolen money or items from the building. They seemingly didn't even try to find the stolen items or money, as they never filed a report. Ironically, it seems that the police profiling and treatment of Ford only pushed him further into the behavior that the police were afraid of.

Kent Ford was born in Louisiana in 1943 and—like many people during this time—his family relocated to California in 1955 for greater opportunities. He became a door-to-door candy salesman and after spending three days in jail for going fifteen miles over the speed limit, he moved to Portland in 1961 and found that Black people bonded over stories of being harassed by the police. He continued to sell candy and became a computer operator for the Safeway chain of grocery stores.

The same year as the break-in to his home, Ford read an article in the *New York Times Magazine* about the Black Panther Party's protest at the Sacramento courthouse. Black Panther cofounder Huey P. Newton had uncovered California case law that made it legal to open carry loaded guns in the state. The Panthers wanted to exercise this right to defend themselves, and to ensure that the police obeyed the law. The Panthers obtained a police radio and would race to the scene with their guns when the police stopped Black people, in order to pressure cops to refrain from violence. In response, Republicans introduced a bill in 1967 to make it illegal to carry a loaded gun in incorporated areas of California. Governor Ronald Reagan spoke against the need for the right to bear arms and signed the bill, granting California some of the strictest gun control in the country. In stark contrast to the civil rights movement, the Black Panthers didn't eschew violence, but rather promised to defend their communities from the state's violence.

With the bill entering legislative proceedings, thirty Panthers showed up in Sacramento, posing with their guns at the state courthouse, knowing they would make national news. In the middle of a speech, Ronald Reagan ran away as the Black Panthers arrived and the media turned their attention to Black Panther cofounder Bobby Seale. Seale gave a televised speech written by Huey P. Newton. In the photos accompanying the article, Ford recognized some people that he had gone to high school with in Richmond, California. He was intrigued and inspired. And he liked their iconic fashion of black leather jackets and berets.

Ford researched the group a bit more. At Kaiser Aerospace & Electronics, a young, former Air Force technician and engineer, Bobby Seale, worked on the Gemini missile program. Then, in 1962, Dr. Martin Luther King Jr. came to speak in Oakland, which taught Seale the mathematics of leverage and social power. Dr. King had spoken about the power of boycotts and community-funded support programs, which inspired Seale to leave engineering for organizing. It was then that Seale met Newton—who had been breaking into cars at the Herrick campus of the Alta Bates Summit Medical Center to make money. Newton had never learned to read or write before entering high school but was determined to find a better life—even if that meant studying law at Merritt College to become a better burglar. Horrified and trying to keep Newton from getting deeper into his life as a career criminal, Seale hired Newton to be his assistant in 1965, organizing businesses and working with the mayor's office. Seale and Newton were two dynamically different people from very different worlds, but they shared a common vision of justice—even if the paths they envisioned were divergent. Oakland's Black population had grown 1200 percent from 1940 to 1960 because of the promises of jobs in the shipyards and factories, but by 1950—like Portland— these jobs were gone and the Black community was faced with police brutality, discrimination, segregation, and poor-quality housing. Seale had been standing up to bullies his whole life, so confronting systemic injustice was just a natural progression.

In Oakland in 1966, Bobby Seale and Huey P. Newton founded the Black Panther Party for Self-Defense, based on the principles of Robert F. Williams and Malcolm X. Seale did the organizing and Newton did the talking. They were a powerful duo that quickly attracted a large following. Stokely Carmichael and Mark Comfort had moved to Oakland from Lowndes County, Alabama and had begun armed patrols of the streets of Oakland to protect Black residents. They would tail the police and post bail for Black people after they were arrested.[15] Seale and Newton took notice and saw the potential in protecting their community. They had become distraught by unenforced laws and with how Black activism was devolving into merely intellectual talk and theory. They wanted to create a popular movement that would appeal to unemployed criminals on the fringes of society and turn them into card-carrying Black intellectuals.

Inspired by Mark Comfort and using Maoist language, Newton and Seale argued that the government was an occupying force upon Black communities that provided inadequate social services, if any. So to help their people, the Black Panther Party needed to create their own system of social services.

Quickly, the duo felt that they should create their own organization. They chose the black panther as a symbol because it was a ferocious animal but didn't attack unless backed into a corner. The Oakland duo met Stokeley Carmichael at a conference in nearby Berkeley. Newton showed Seale the logo from the Lowndes County Black Panther Party. They adopted the name and iconography. Blending theory and practice, Seale showed Newton the works of Frantz Fanon, Robert F. Williams, James Baldwin, and W.E.B. Du Bois—writers that they considered vital to their struggle. They created a Ten-Point Program for their goals that they published in the first issue of their newspaper:

1. We Want Freedom. We Want Power To
    Determine The Destiny Of Our Black
    Community.

---

15 Police in Oakland in 1966 were 96 percent white men relocated from the South while the city was 50 percent non-white.

2. We Want Full Employment For Our People.

3. We Want An End To The Robbery By The Capitalists Of Our Black Community.

4. We Want Decent Housing Fit For The Shelter Of Human Beings.

5. We Want Education For Our People That Exposes The True Nature Of This Decadent American Society. We Want Education That Teaches Us Our True History And Our Role In The Present-Day Society.

6. We Want All Black Men To Be Exempt From Military Service.

7. We Want An Immediate End To Police Brutality And Murder Of Black People.

8. We Want Freedom For All Black Men Held In Federal, State, County, And City Prisons And Jails.

9. We Want All Black People, When Brought To Trial, To Be Tried In Court By A Jury Of Their Peer Group Or People From Their Black Communities, As Defined By The Constitution Of The United States.

10. We Want Land, Bread, Housing, Education, Clothing, Justice, And Peace.

Immediately, they began attracting members and believers—almost all of whom were born in the South and had relocated to Oakland. They fundraised through selling copies of Mao's 1964 "little red book" on the Berkeley campus. They joked that they had sold quite a few of them before they opened a copy and read it, thinking it was pretty good. They primarily used the money to buy guns to protect their communities. Richard Aoki, an army veteran who spent time in a Japanese internment camp, began donating guns to the group as well.[16]

The Panthers stood up to police and stated the letter of the law. Eldridge Cleaver witnessed Newton tell a gang of police officers that if they did anything with their guns, he would have no choice but to shoot them. This was a stark contrast to the long-held relationship between Black people and the police. When the Panthers did this, the community saw police back down for the first time. Cleaver was impressed and joined the group. The Panthers would perform their own murder investigations, in one case showing that a 22-year-old had been shot six times with his arms raised in surrender— the police lied in the report, trying to make the murder seem necessary. When a car killed a child in a dangerous intersection and the city refused to do anything, the Panthers performed crossing guard duties until the city was humiliated into installing a traffic light.

As the Black Panthers started to gain momentum, they began publishing their own newspaper[17] with the art of Emory Douglas. Black Panther chapters in other cities could purchase and sell these newspapers to leftists who were supportive of the cause. This strategy can be traced back to communists in the '20s, as an early form of fundraising while simultaneously

---

16 In 2007 and after his suicide in 2009, numerous FBI documents were uncovered, painting an elaborate picture that Aoki was actually informing on Newton and Seale to the FBI as early as 1966.

17 The *Black Panther* was published for fourteen years, with a total of 537 issues and a weekly circulation reaching three hundred thousand.

spreading their message. Panther membership quickly grew to the hundreds. Notable Black Panthers include singer Chaka Khan, actor Samuel L. Jackson, and TV personality Judge Joe Brown. They successfully radicalized gangsters with a history of police skirmishes to become their security force. By recruiting members who were already trained with guns and comfortable with confrontation, they did not need to train members—only to maintain order in the group and community at large. By 1969, numerous other organizations using the name "Black Panther Party" had either disbanded or rebranded and the Oakland group came to the fore.

Police surveillance photo of Sandra Ford, 1970, courtesy of Portland City Archive

Portland Archives, A2004-005.2957

DISPARATE FACES OF REVOLUTION

*T*n 1967, an Oakland police officer recognized Huey P. Newton's car from a previous interaction. The officer, who already had a laundry list of racist behavior in less than two years on the force, decided to confront Newton again. Newton had been up all night partying and was amped up. Much of what happened during that traffic stop will remain a mystery, but the official report claims that the officer shot Newton, then the same officer's gun was used to shoot both officers on the scene. The gun was never recovered and there was no evidence that Newton shot them—though most people drew their own conclusions. Yet, while in the emergency room for his bullet wound, Newton was allegedly handcuffed and beaten by police officers. One of the officers involved in the traffic stop died, and Newton was charged with both shootings. Sensing this as a classic story of injustice, Kent Ford and his friends were on the forefront of the "Free Huey" campaign, which quickly became international. While many details are unclear, the officers had undoubtedly instigated the confrontation and white anti-war protesters of all stripes felt that the state was using Newton as an example to intimidate them. Challenging the status quo was the order of the day for activists, so this injustice could not stand.

Newton was in prison when Dr. Martin Luther King Jr. was assassinated. It was a tremendous loss felt by Black people across all political spectrums. People began to riot and burn cities all over the United states. Seale tried to convince the Party to be strategic, but Eldridge Cleaver and Stokely Carmichael said that it was time to take up arms. Simultaneously, Newton was going through a metamorphosis behind bars and, changing his position, told the Panthers to refrain from violence.

Cleaver had other ideas. Three days after Dr. King's assassination, against the will of Black Panther Party leadership, Cleaver put together a renegade task force with the intent to manufacture an armed confrontation and murder a police officer in Oakland. Instead, the police snuck up on Cleaver while he was urinating on the side of the road. "Lil' Bobby" Hutton and Cleaver fled into a nearby house and engaged in a ninety-minute shoot-out with the police. The police set fire to the house with a smoke bomb. Intending to surrender, Hutton and Cleaver took off their clothes to show they were unarmed and exited the home. Instead, having trouble breathing and falling to his knees, seventeen-year-old Hutton was gunned down by at least six[18] police bullets with his arms raised in surrender. Hutton was still a child and, despite being the first recruit of the Black Panther Party for Self-Defense, he was caught up in an ill-conceived plan. His death remains a terrible tragedy. The public saw this too. Marlon Brando spoke at his funeral in support of the Panthers. The Party was evolving. Public support was growing. The FBI—who had long restrained Black civil rights movements—was watching with great interest as it worked to figure out how to interfere.

The FBI was taken over by J. Edgar Hoover in 1924. It was created in 1908 to operate as a national police force for the Department of Justice when crimes crossed over state lines.

18 Six or twelve bullets, depending whom you believe.

After incorporating forensic science in detective work during the failed effort to recover the ransomed twenty-month-old Lindbergh baby, Hoover's vision for the FBI became more egotistical and much more devious. Eschewing any oversight or transparency into his programs, he compartmentalized the bureau. Agents weren't privy to the bigger picture, only the specific "need to know" information needed to perform their duties. Plans were developed in such a way that even the agents working on the cases could not see Hoover's goals—which further kept the public in the dark.

By 1956, Hoover took this a step further and decided that he should singlehandedly determine who the political enemies of the United States were. He used taxpayer money to dismantle and harass his perceived enemies of the state, again without any government or democratic oversight. Hoover's social values were already severely outdated by this time. He was born in 1895, lived with his mother until he was 43 years old, leaned far to the right, and was a closeted gay man in a relationship with both his fixer Roy Cohn[19] and his assistant, Clyde Tolson. Hoover was a volatile cocktail of self-hatred. He was highly secretive and his outdated worldview slowly led him to see his purpose as undermining any social or cultural change in the United States. He worked relentlessly

19 A slimy, socially connected lawyer for Joseph McCarthy who created careful strategies so that he never had to pay for anything and could make others pay for his lifestyle. His friends tell great stories of how tedious it was to visit a restaurant or art auction with him, because they knew that they could not return to those establishments. He hid all of his money in shell corporations, maintained tenuous relationships with gossip reporters, and went on to teach Donald Trump everything he knows. Cohn can often be seen next to J. Edgar Hoover in photographs from the time but rarely identified in textbooks because of his unofficial and underhanded role in history. See the 2020 documentary, *Bully. Coward. Victim: The Story of Roy Cohn* for further information.

with Joseph McCarthy to publicly embarrass closeted queer people working in Hollywood, government jobs, and elected officials. McCarthy, Cohn, and Hoover identified their own political enemies as "communists," and made it impossible for them to find work in their field.[20]

In 1956, he formalized these efforts as the FBI's COINTELPRO. Many film stars were blacklisted from the profession by Hoover and had to seek out other work. The blacklist project was so effective that it eventually backfired— Congressman John Moss started asking questions about the thousands of federal employees that Eisenhower fired for being "communists" and asked to see the associated records for their terminations. Moss created a congressional subcommittee on government information in 1955 and by 1966, he created the Freedom of Information Act, wherein any citizen could pose a question that the government would have to answer. Moss's fear was that Eisenhower's decree to terminate thousands of people without cause fundamentally resembled that of a dictatorship. The sheer volume of instances of the government creeping to the right during this era concerned the public as well.

Simultaneously, Hoover's COINTELPRO operation to identify and undermine "communists" was so successful that he expanded it to other leftist organizations working for social change. So, when Dr. Martin Luther King Jr. spoke out against the war in Vietnam, Hoover was outraged. He began a relentless campaign to undermine, dismantle, and destroy the civil rights movement. By 1967, in addition to

20 The Portland Police Union was instrumental in proposing a resolution for the House Un-American Activities Committee to investigate Hollywood producers for making films glamorizing '30s mobsters, contributing to the second "Red Scare."

registration campaigns for Black voters, Hoover was obsessed with the Black Power movement. By 1968, the Black Panther Party for Self-Defense was on his radar as well and Hoover was desperately paranoid about the "rise of a Black messiah." Exactly a month before the assassination of Dr. King, Hoover sent a memo detailing the need to dismantle "an effective coalition of Black nationalist groups." Hoover saw the unity of Black people as the greatest threat to the United States, specifically identifying Stokely Carmichael and Dr. Martin Luther King Jr. as powerful threats because of their ability to unite Black people. Hoover identified the key to preventing these leaders from establishing prominence was by discrediting their "respectability."

The irony, of course, is that Hoover and Tolson were protecting actual criminals while harassing the left. They would take vacations in mob-owned hotels and make the FBI pay for them. When the mob blackmailed Hoover with compromising photos of himself and Tolson, Hoover began claiming there was no organized crime in the United States, even though he was personally affiliated with a number of mob bosses.

Building off of Roy Cohn's strategy of feeding news stories to the media about people he wanted to influence or smear, Hoover took this a step further. The FBI had much greater resources and escalated the tactic by funding and creating their own newspapers.[21] COINTELPRO went into the business of reporting on stories about their enemies

---

21 Kent Ford made claims that a newspaper in Portland was founded with COINTELPRO funds but the newspaper was able to show me evidence that contradicted Ford's claims.

without any truth or evidence and adjusting facts to suit their narratives.

In 1971, during the Muhammad Ali vs. Joe Frazier fight,[22] a physics professor and eight associates broke into an FBI field office in Media, Pennsylvania after becoming suspicious that the FBI was spying on civilians.[23] They called themselves the Citizens' Commission to Investigate the FBI. The group decided that the best way to confirm their fears was to prove them. What they found not only confirmed their suspicions but proved far greater horrors to be true. Only 40 percent of the FBI's efforts were spent on crime. The other 60 percent was spent on people that Hoover was politically opposed to. The group found documentation about decades of illegal spying on activist organizations, in direct contradiction to the First Amendment. The FBI falsely accused anyone that Hoover didn't like of crimes and hired prostitutes with STIs to seduce their political enemies with the intention of destroying their reputation. Extensive surveillance of the Black community showed that the FBI had planted informants in barber shops, churches, taxis, community colleges, and apartment buildings. A shockingly intense campaign against Black America was intent on creating fear amongst Black Americans to "enhance paranoia."[24] Law-abiding citizens asking questions that Hoover didn't like would be subjected to an intense campaign of harassment, including agents visiting their friends, relatives, and neighbors.

22 To anyone who contends that sports are not political, I offer that sports are a spectacular distraction when planning activities such as this.
23 *The Burglary: The Discovery of J. Edgar Hoover's Secret FBI* and check out the interview with all involved on podcasts.apple.com/us/podcast/criminal/id809264944?i=1000552202100
24 *The COINTELPRO Papers*, Ward Churchill, South End Press, 2001

The break-in story was buried, but Hoover was apoplectic, sending two hundred agents to investigate it. However, the FBI failed to solve the crime—the greatest proof that they are not a crime-fighting organization, but a vehicle to destroy Hoover's political enemies. The group took every document in the office and sent them to reporters at the *New York Times*, *Washington Post*, and *Los Angeles Times*, plus two members of Congress. Everyone but the *Washington Post* immediately forwarded the documents to the FBI. However, journalist Betty Medsger began verifying the accuracy in the documents while the attorney general began demanding that the *Washington Post* not publish their findings. It is only because of these American heroes that we ever learned about how our government was violating its own laws. Leadership at the *Washington Post* was opposed to running Medsger's article, but the article ran because her editor pointed out that the greatest danger in these findings was to the Black community, not to the government.

Indeed, Hoover described the Black Panther social programs such as the free clinics and free breakfasts as "the most dangerous" because they were "indoctrinating Black youth." One FBI memo claimed that the Panthers' breakfast program's real purpose was to "poison the minds of ghetto children with anti-white propaganda" and "indoctrinate youngsters with hate and violence." Hoover was particularly concerned about youth recruitment, as he correctly saw this as the future of these movements. Without supporting evidence—because they don't need any—the FBI deemed the Panthers as the organization most "prone" to violence. Their marching orders: dismantle the Black Panther Party *through any means necessary.*[25]

25 *The COINTELPRO Papers*, Ward Churchill, South End Press, 2001

After the shoot-out with police and the disastrous outcome of his ill-conceived plan, Eldridge Cleaver was brought up on charges of attempted murder and preexisting warrants. When someone posted his bail, he fled to the communist nation of Cuba to avoid extradition. But even Fidel Castro was hearing about how COINTELPRO had infiltrated members of the Black Panther Party. After the CIA had coordinated the equally disastrous Bay of Pigs invasion of Cuba in 1961, Castro had plenty of reasons to be wary. Fearing that Cleaver may be a CIA plant, Castro asked him to leave, so Cleaver met up with his wife, Kathleen Cleaver, and fled to Algeria. The country had recently won independence from France, which meant that Cleaver could not be extradited. The Cleavers would go on to create a stronghold for other Panthers hiding from the U.S. government. The Algerian government even granted the Cleavers a stipend and the Black Panthers were given an embassy.

The Black Panther Party was facing a lot of turmoil and rapidly changing as leadership figured out its ideal strategic role. It would be several years before it clearly found its footing.

BRINGING INSPIRATION HOME

*B*ack in Portland, tensions flared again in 1969. A restaurant owner contacted Kent Ford, saying that he witnessed police clubbing Black teenagers for loitering. Ford had taken on an informal role of mediating neighborhood problems. A few days later, Ford and two friends were driving south on what is now NE Martin Luther King Boulevard.[26] They saw some children rolling dice in a restaurant parking lot and being hassled by cops for curfew violations. They stopped and tried to intervene, insisting to the police that they would get all of the kids home safely to their parents. But the cops continued harassing the kids. Without thinking, Ford opened the back door of a police cruiser to release the ten-year-old kid the police had arrested, telling him to run home. Six officers immediately surrounded Ford, maced him, and arrested him. According to reporting in the *Oregonian*, the children started to riot, beating up a cop with their bare hands and popping all four tires of the car Ford was arrested in. The *Oregon Journal* similarly reported on "the disturbance, during which policemen were kicked, beaten, and struck with thrown objects." The cops stated that "[Officer] Hegge said he was struck in the head from behind and knocked partially unconscious." Another claimed that his badge was torn from his uniform. In the police's version of events, they somehow barely escaped with their lives and traveled five blocks on four flat tires. The sheer unlikelihood that these children were able to overtake the officers aside, Ford denies that any of this <u>sensationalism is</u> factual. Accounts agree that Ford was pulled

26 In 1969, it was called "Union Ave."

into a McDonald's parking lot where forty more police officers had congregated. One officer noticed Ford was attempting to swallow some cannabis. As the officer put his finger into Ford's throat, he bit down hard, and the officers beat Ford thoroughly. They brought Ford's bloody body downtown to central booking on charges of "rioting." The officers alleged that Ford was shouting "Get whitey" and "Let's kill those white . . . pigs!" as well as providing profanity-laden encouragement to the "mob." In jail, bruised and bloodied, Ford asked the city's sole Black cop, "How can you work for them when they treat our people like this?"

Unrelated to the dice game in the parking lot, there were eleven additional arrests that night. It seems like Kent Ford was being associated with a certain amount of chaos from out-of-control partying during the Rose Festival. In reviewing police after-action reports, this is common. If a fur protest happens

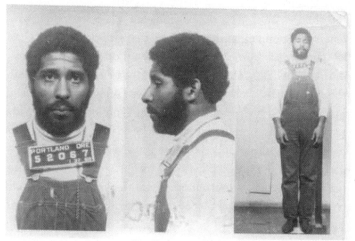

Kent Ford arrest photos, 1969

on the same day as a bike ride, both reports go in the same folder and the police think they are related. It does seem like things were wild on this particular night. Apparently, someone pulled a driver out of his moving cab and the car went through the window of a furniture store. However, none of the chaos seems related to Kent Ford or the kids in the parking lot.

The following Saturday and Sunday, cops drove around—some allegedly drunk—with their license plates covered and no badges.[27] The police let loose all of their frustration over the incident with Ford and the previous weekend by beating up random people in Albina, including women and the local newspaper editor.[28] When a TV cameraman showed up, the police told him to leave. A total of 136 more people were arrested, none of them police officers.

After getting bailed out in June by Don Hamerquist,[29] a sympathetic white Reed College student, Ford made a speech on the steps of the justice center, declaring in June, "If they keep coming in with these fascist tactics, we're going to defend ourselves." Ford then approached the human relations director

27 It is unclear if all of the police admit that they removed their badges knowingly or claim that their badges were removed against their will by children, similar to the incident in the parking lot.

28 Jimmy "Bang-Bang" Walker was taking photos of the police brutality so the police exposed his roll of film and left him with injuries that hospitalized him for days.

29 Hamerquist went on to write *Confronting Fascism: Discussion Documents for a Militant Movement*. The bail fund was created in response to events in 1936, when the German Navy flew the Nazi flag in Portland for the first time. The United States then regarded Germany as our ally but as Portlanders cheered for the Nazis, eleven protesters, including three Reed students, were arrested for "flying banners without permits." Arresting the few people protesting Nazis in Portland led to the creation of a bail fund at Reed for acts of righteous indignation.

of the city. During their meeting, the director proclaimed "They must have thought you were a Black Panther or something!" then proceeded to ignore Ford for months. Perhaps in defiance, Ford and his friends began referring to themselves as Black Panthers, even though they did not have permission to use that designation. In addition to Huey P. Newton being in prison and the future of the organization in question, the national Black Panther office was overwhelmed by an incredible demand for permission to create local Black Panther chapters. Nonetheless, Ford and his friends could count on the half dozen people in their ranks and formed the backbone of an organization.

•　　•　　•

Over Ford's ten-day trial, his attorney, Nick Chaivoe, successfully overturned the police narrative that Ford had instigated the violence. When his attorney subpoenaed tapes of the police radio to show that Ford arrived after the incident, the tapes went missing. The Black jailer testified about Ford's condition after being arrested. When the judge found out that Ford had been handcuffed at the time of his savage beating by the cops, the rioting charges were dropped and he was acquitted by an all-white jury.[30] In the following civil trial, Ford was awarded $7,000[31] for "indignities suffered" and "punitive damages" for the beating, with the judge declaring, "The people of the community cannot be expected to have confidence in the government until the government's officers act fairly and according to law towards all members of the community."

30 The original jury panel included the sister of future Black Panther Oscar Johnson who wrote speeches for Floyd Cruse. She was removed from the jury, not because of her conflict of interest—having a relationship with Kent Ford—but because she was Black.

31 About $45,000 today.

It was the first time that someone associated with the Black Panther Party was awarded damages for their treatment at the hands of police anywhere in the United States. Allegedly, Ford's home later received a phone call from the jury foreman to say that "not all white people hate you all." A more looming truth was the likelihood of police retaliation, for which even Ford's white lawyer warned him.

Nonetheless, emboldened by this early victory, Ford and his neighbors continued running into each other and began organizing community meetings around political education in their neighborhood. They raised bail money for people they believed were being targeted by the police. For fourteen months, they had private book study groups, focusing on global and local political movements and histories. They hosted discussions of praxis, like, "What is the best practice if one of us is arrested? What do you say? Who do you contact?" Like the actual Black Panthers, they envisioned themselves as working-class intellectuals who took an active role in determining the direction of their lives and communities. They took to heart Bobby Seale's message that Black Panthers should read two hours every day. When I asked early recruit Percy Hampton in 2022 if this intellectualism contradicts the Panthers' reputation of iconic paramilitarism, he sat with the question for a moment before declaring, "A lot of the guys and gals were the nerdy kind! I was still in high school," before explaining, "I got involved with the Black Muslims but they were a racist organization. When my mom found out that I got involved with Kent, it scared her. So I said, 'I'm going to get involved with something. [The police] are going to do anything they can to make us look bad. This is the best option out there.'" Indeed, what good options does someone have under conditions like these? Talking to Hampton clarified something that I hadn't considered: when growing up in an occupied, racist state, each person has a choice to either get in line with the status quo and try to blend in or join the fomenting revolution. As a teenager, Hampton was an intelligent idealist; he wanted his cake and to eat it too. He sought more than protection—he wanted politics that reflected his own values in a group. He wanted to better himself and knew that the state didn't have his best interests at heart. As a sixteen-year-old, the Panthers were both a safety net and a way to create the world Hampton wanted to live in.

Speaking to the fears of Hampton's mother, Richard Nixon indicated that Hoover was not doing enough to dismantle the Panthers, despite 279 of his 295 COINTELPRO actions against Black nationalists targeting the Black Panthers. Nixon had campaigned on a platform of "law and order" and wanted the FBI to provide additional resources to local police to dismantle the Panthers. They often used paid informants holding high-ranking positions within the Black Panther Party to escalate confrontation with the police. Seemingly, they had no limits.

In a move that bears no resemblance to "law and order," the FBI sent letters seeking to instigate a conflict between the Los Angeles Panthers and their rivals until violence broke out in January 1969. Documents imply that the people who killed Bunchy Carter and John Huggins, the leaders of the chapter, were informants carrying out directives from the FBI.[32] A memo attributes the situation—and thus the murders—to COINTELPRO. The Panther's successor, Geronimo Pratt, was framed on murder charges with falsified evidence and an FBI informant as a witness, even though FBI records show

32 David F. Walker and Marcus Kwame Anderson, *The Black Panther Party: A Graphic Novel History* (Ten Speed Press, 2021).

officers' knowledge of Pratt's innocence.[33] These incidents remain a horrifying escalation—just like what the CIA had done to Lumumba in the Congo. Hoover even considered murder to be acceptable to achieve the goals of the United States. Hoover's imperative to prevent the Black Panthers from "gaining respectability" seemingly knew no bounds.

Percy Hampton's high school senior photo, courtesy of Percy Hampton

Before long, Ford's private study group in Portland had grown to about twenty members. Recognizing the heat all over the country, they were quiet and kept a low profile. Hampton explained to Martha Gies and Jules Boykoff, "We never did openly display our weapons . . . we kept focused on the issues and [kept] the violence and rhetoric down." Ford clarified to me, "We didn't want to be picked off too easily," both to recognize that the state had all advantages and that violence was never the goal. They didn't want to be perceived as "out of control radicals" because it went against their objectives. The police responded by hassling the people who attended these meetings and the residents of Albina. Hampton, who was still a

33 Geronimo Pratt's conviction was vacated after 27 years in 1997 when it became clear that he was framed by the FBI and they were aware that he was not in town during the murder.

bespectacled Catholic school–educated teenager, recalls being arrested while walking to the store by his house, in a situation that escalated quickly from insults and ended with him being charged with disorderly conduct, resisting arrest, and assaulting a police officer. His mistake? Correcting the officers, saying that he was "not a boy, but a young man." Two weeks later, he was unexpectedly released but the message was clear: we are watching you and we have the power to disrupt your future.

Kent Ford went to hear a speech at Portland State College[34] from the head of the Seattle Black Panthers—the first chapter founded outside of California. Ford was again inspired and intended to start his own Black Panther Party chapter in Portland, but with Huey P. Newton in prison, the Party was in transition and reevaluating their priorities. The Black Panthers had grown exponentially over the past three years and were not currently accepting new branches. Instead, as the Oakland Black Panthers recommended, Ford founded a chapter of the National Committee to Combat Fascism (NCCF), but the Portlanders began using Black Panther iconography, sloganeering, and images on their flyers. The media began referring to them as "Black Panthers" immediately, and so did their own membership. So from here on out, they are referred to informally as Portland's Black Panthers except where noted. For an office, they shared a rented house with anti-war organizers, The Resistance, and began to oscillate referring to themselves as the NCCF or "Black Panthers," as this seemed to be how they saw themselves immediately. In a 2005 interview, Floyd Cruse stated that he got involved with the Black Panthers when he received a letter in the mail. He viewed it similarly to his military draft, explaining, "It was saying, 'your community

34 The following year the school became "Portland State University."

needs you to protect it.'" And he accepted the call. Cruse recounted how, even in Albina, Black people felt disconnected from each other. He explained that the Panthers felt like a way to stand strong together and challenge that. Cruse was a musician and performer, so he brought those skills to the Party, becoming the speaker and deputy minister of information for the group, performing speeches written by Panther researcher and assistant deputy minister of Information Oscar Johnson, and giving interviews to the press. Cruse explained how each person brought their talents to the movement and made it stronger. Yet, almost immediately, the FBI and Portland Police began illegally surveilling the NCCF office through nearly every possible means.

Unlike other chapters, the Portland Panthers did not attempt to intimidate police. Perhaps it was the public opinion and national news stories circulating around these issues, but the NCCF put their effort into public awareness about police behavior. When I asked each Panther why they chose social service over display of arms years before the national party moved in this direction, I was told over and over how many violent cops there were in Portland and how few Black people. In many ways, the membership knew that violence was a losing proposition against such odds—both in the streets and in the media. In this way, the Portland NCCF was forward thinking and other chapters looked to them for direction. Instead of fighting in the streets, they sat in during court cases involving Black people and made a list of which judges and lawyers they deemed to be white supremacists, posting them on Albina telephone poles. Their group recognized the value of progressive community activism, and membership continued to grow to a few dozen people.

Four months after his trial, the police arrested Ford again for "disorderly conduct." He had seen a fire in the distance and walked over with some neighbors to take a look. Apparently, some of the ovens at Grandma's Cookies had caught fire, but it was unclear at the time. A police officer onsite accused Ford of setting the fire and Ford was arrested. In an interview, when I implied that Ford shouted at the police officer, he was very clear, "I didn't shout at the police officer! I called him a pig and the N-word!" He claims that the police attempted to convince a man facing twenty years to say that Ford was responsible for the fire, explaining, "If they can't turn you, they can't use you." But the man did not cooperate with the police. The media speculated that Ford's $1,000 bail was the highest ever set for this offense, yet, he was only sentenced to six months probation. Soon thereafter, fourteen people—including Ford—filed a class-action lawsuit against specific police officers, the mayor, city council, and the police chief on account of the harsh police enforcement and profiling imposed on Black residents. Gradually, the attorney found more and more people who had been mistreated at the hands of Portland Police and the suit came to represent twenty thousand residents of Portland.

A major notable aspect about Kent Ford is his endless advocacy and ability to use the system to defend his rights and those of his community. I've been beaten by cops on a number of occasions and it would never have occurred to me to attempt to use the justice system to hold police accountable for their actions because it tends to only work in one direction. Of course, this is what misbehaving cops prey upon and the NCCF weren't putting up with it. It's an interesting development because, while the Panthers' paramilitaristic reputation would lead you to expect something more sweeping than police reform in the courts, the measure did some of what it intended to.

The suit resulted in the Probasco Decree. Police were required to stop using "insulting, degrading, or ethnically derogatory terms." Police were required to cease beating people with batons and "SAP gloves," which are basically neutered brass knuckles. Police were also required to obtain a search warrant before entering a home. Shockingly, despite the Portland Police's scandals of the '50s, there was no Internal Affairs Division and so the Black Panthers forced the city to create one in order to monitor the bad behavior of their own organization.

These felt like substantial accomplishments, but when I asked Ford how he felt about it, he laughed and said, "Probasco was just another neoliberal show." I take his point. Internal Affairs rejected 90–93 percent of complaints they received each year for the next decade. But the revelations that Probasco revealed were also shocking. One officer testified about the incredible volume of cocaine that his fellow officers removed from evidence and consumed before conducting drug raids. When the same officer investigated the murder of a drug dealer, he filed a scathing report to the chief implicating fellow officers, claiming they had murdered the man and staged his suicide. When the officer later requested a copy of his own report, Internal Affairs informed him that it was never filed because it had been immediately shredded. When the mother of the man who was allegedly murdered pursued an investigation into her son's death, she received a phone call instructing her to back off unless she wanted "more family members dead."

Internal Affairs launched an investigation into the wrongful death of an officer that illuminated police corruption in the drug unit, and resulted in charges of planting drugs on innocent people and consumption of evidence. This led to the resignation of two officers, including one officer who was found to be purchasing and reselling drugs from suspects. After a period of investigation, 59 cases were found with falsified evidence, 35 additional cases were being overturned because of bogus evidence, and nearly 100 cases were immediately overturned. One case was overturned in which there was sufficient evidence to prove that a dealer had killed a police officer. The dealer was released from prison because the officers had lied on the stand.

It's difficult to understand how police behavior could be this unruly while officers were confident that there would be no consequences, and there is similar behavior to this day. As Hampton told me, "Portland had plenty of thumper cops . . . the same issues as the rest of the U.S. . . . police who liked to beat on us and wanted to put us in jail." So, while Ford is quick to downplay the effectiveness of Probasco, it does seem that it tempered police behavior and at least forced them to get better at covering up reprehensible behavior.

A PARTY OF PROGRAMS

*W*ith Huey P. Newton in prison and Eldridge Cleaver on the run, Black Panther Party cofounder Bobby Seale created "Serve the People"[35] programs in the Fall of 1968. The services were an extension of the original Ten-Point Program and sought to create social services for those in need that the government was turning a blind eye to. First, the Panthers would establish free breakfast programs to feed Black youth, providing them with the means to succeed in school and elsewhere. Then they would establish community control of the police to reign in their violent tendencies. Next, they would establish community free clinics and their own Black liberation schools. These programs were important, not only to support their neighborhoods, but to counter government propaganda that the Black Panthers were a violent organization. By this point in their history, most press about the Panthers, including in the *Oregonian* and *Oregon Journal*, depicted them as violent perpetrators that sought shoot-outs with the police. In November, 1968, the *Oregon Journal* wrote that the Black Panther Party wants, "ghetto rebellions, which they believe will lead to anarchy and revolution," even though the Party didn't yet exist in Oregon and the premise of the story was completely false. When an organization is dedicated to social change, misbehaving members like Eldridge Cleaver, who did what he wanted despite the edicts of the organization, are portrayed as the norm when they are outliers.

---

35 In 1971, these were rebranded as "Community Survival" programs.

Recognizing the same imperatives as Seale and Newton, Portland's Black Panthers wanted to help their community heal from the distrust of the medical establishment, learn about their own health, and live long, prosperous lives. In a 2022 interview, Ford explained that the Portland chapter was looking at the national Black Panther Party and shifting their approach based on the direction that they expected things to go. They were correct in predicting this shift toward service programs.

In 1969, with a few dozen members, the first projects of the Portland Black Panthers were opening a dental clinic, a free health clinic, and a free breakfast program for anyone who couldn't afford these services. When asked why they performed social services, Kent Ford told Dr. Judson L. Jeffries, "The government had money to fight a war thousands and thousands of miles away . . . and send astronauts to the moon, but ensuring that kids received a well-balanced meal before heading off to school was not a priority . . . so the Panthers made it a priority." It was a clever ploy; by demonstrating how social services could be offered without a federal budget, the Panthers could pressure others to do the same.

For the 1969/70 school year, the Portland Panthers began serving free breakfast at Highland United Church of Christ on NE Ninth Avenue at Going Street. The Panthers knew they would be challenged at every turn, so they chose the church not only for its size and location near Dr. Martin Luther King Jr. Elementary School, but also because it had recently passed fire and health code inspections. They obtained food handlers cards while local people and businesses donated food and labor. It was not difficult to demonstrate the need to feed the community's most vulnerable. In Oakland, political education was combined with breakfast, whereas in Portland, they knew that offering breakfast with no strings attached would go further to make the community appreciate them. During a 2022 walking tour, I asked Ford why he didn't combine breakfast with political education like they did in Oakland and he refuted that while they had books available about Black history onsite, the minister of the church where they cooked had a heart, yet gave the Party explicit instructions not to cause trouble.

Within a year the Portland Panthers fed 75–125 children daily. The principal of Dr. Martin Luther King King Jr. Elementary School admitted in the press, "The Panthers serve a much better breakfast than we do." When reporters for the Lewis & Clark student newspaper attended the breakfast, they were surprised to find that there was no talk of politics and the children ate all of the food on their plates. It was a downright orderly affair, fulfilling the ambitious goals that the Panthers set out to achieve. The breakfast was not only healthier than the one served at the school, it was free and better attended. When asked when they would stop, Ford responded, "When the government steps forward and give[s] our people a balanced diet, we'll be glad to stop." Indeed, the Panthers effectively embarrassed the federal government into carrying out their agenda. In the Portland Police files on the Panthers, I found an article in the *Vanguard* from January 8, 1971, where Portland State University student groups voted to donate money to the Black Panthers breakfast program and administrators attempted to find legal channels to prevent this, claiming it was not "for the educational benefit of the institution where [donations] were collected." The students vowed to give the money to the breakfast program, "legally or illegally," and the police informants were attempting to leverage this incident as "proof" that the Panthers were up to no good. Yet, people came out of the woodwork. Ford fondly recalls how the main cook stepped forward to contribute and the volunteering helped the cook to get his drinking under control. They purchased bulk food from wholesalers and got to work at 5:00 a.m. every day. Over the next five years, the federal government increased its free school breakfast program fivefold. To this day, former students thank Portland's Black Panthers for providing them with a healthy breakfast over fifty years ago.

When a local used clothing store went out of business, the owners gave all of their inventory to the NCCF and turned over the lease to them. For $100 a month, the Portland Panthers suddenly had a free clothing pickup spot for their community. While this location didn't last even a whole year and the NCCF had trouble sourcing a sufficient quantity of used clothes, it was another way in which they emboldened their role in the community and operated as a social center in their neighborhood.

In 1970, Jon Moscow, a Panther supporter, suggested opening a free clinic. After bailing Ford out in 1969, Don Hamerquist had introduced him to Moscow. Hamerquist and Moscow are both white, though they recognized and valued the aims of the Panthers and established ways to work towards common goals.

Jon Moscow's interest in opening a clinic was an extension of his work with Health Research Action Project (Health/RAP). Health/RAP was a spinoff of the national organization

Health/PAC,[36] and they specialized in demonstrating how Portland healthcare is complicit in oppressing the poor. Moscow recognized the immense neglect that Black people received in healthcare—and saw an opportunity to embarrass the city. Moscow gave Ford a list of every doctor he knew that would be willing to volunteer for the Panthers' clinic. Next, he sought out necessary equipment and permits.

Based on the Haight Ashbury Free Clinic created for peaceniks who turned up in San Francisco during 1967, the Portland group created the Fred Hampton Memorial People's Health Clinic on the northeast corner of Vancouver Avenue at Russell Street. The clinic was named after Fred Hampton, the eighteen-year-old head of the Chicago chapter who established the first "rainbow coalitions."[37] He had been radicalized when he was framed for the robbery of an ice cream truck[38] and was slated to become the national speaker for the Black Panther Party while the previous leadership was either in prison or exile. Instead, he was murdered in his sleep by the FBI in 1969.[39] The FBI made no effort to disguise,

36 Whose work is conveniently archived at healthpacbulletin.org/1987/

37 Rainbow coalitions are groups of disparate but intersectional groups working together due to their shared experiences of oppression. Fred Hampton successfully organized Chicago's rival gangs to work together. To interfere with this alliance, the FBI told gang leaders that the Black Panthers were trying to kill them. The concept and phrase of "rainbow coalitions" was later adopted by Jesse Jackson.

38 The original reporting on this appeared in Michael Hoerger, Mia Partlow, and Nate Powell's *Edible Secrets: A Food Tour of Classified U.S. History*, 2010.

39 The FBI paid $17,000 to the Party's treasurer, head of security, and one of Hampton's "best friends," William O'Neil, who drugged Hampton's drink and provided a map and information. The 3:00 a.m. raid was led by Daniel Groth, a rumored CIA plant, and the investigation by U.S. Attorney General Ramsey Clark found that the police had fired first and fired about one hundred bullets despite people inside the house begging them to cease,

explain, or excuse the brutality of his murder. Naming the clinic after him was a stark reminder of the lengths that the FBI was willing to go in order to prevent justice for Black people.

Due to the clinic spawning from Moscow's personal network, it incorporated numerous other key white allies who were doctors, funders, and advocates, intensely aware of the lack of healthcare available to poor and Black people. In addition, there simply were not many Black doctors or healthcare professionals to begin with, let alone ones who had the time to volunteer with the clinic and could face the scrutiny and heat for assisting the Black Panthers.

With a stenciled sign in the window, the clinic opened from 7:00–10:00 p.m. every night and saw patients quickly, without asking questions, and without insurance or judgment. They helped as many impoverished white patients as they did Black ones because they recognized the shared oppression and struggle of those living in poverty.

The Fred Hampton Memorial People's Health Clinic was primarily the project of Sandra Ford, who married Kent Ford in June 1970. Sandra Ford and Jon Moscow relentlessly contacted doctors to ask them to volunteer, cleaned up between appointments, made sure everyone was in their place and comfortable, and ensured that people could get the care they desperately needed. When patients couldn't get themselves to the clinic, the NCCF did that as well. Between the Black-owned Rose City Cab Company and their own volunteers, they would pick up patients as part of their daily activities.

including a pregnant woman. No action was ever taken against the officers.

In 1972, when the national Black Panther Party decreed that all branches must offer free healthcare for Black and oppressed people, Portland already had the most functional and advanced system in the country. By this point, Portland's public county clinics were referring white patients to the Fred Hampton Memorial People's Health Clinic for superior care. The Panthers were—once again—doing a better job of providing essential social services than the government. Each doctor could help up to 35 patients nightly. Featuring a staff of virtually all white volunteer doctors, they also touted some celebrities, including Lendon Smith, the "Children's Doctor," an author and TV personality on late-night shows. Smith doubled as the publicity arm of the Fred Hampton Memorial People's Health Clinic and would frequently promote it in the media and within his professional circles. When the Panthers couldn't give a patient everything they needed, they had specialists that they could refer them to for free. For outreach they held BBQs where they spread information about breast cancer, sickle cell anemia, and lead poisoning. The clinic focused extensively on awareness and preventative care as they recognized this could help the largest number of people with the smallest amount of effort.

The Black Panther Party viewed sickle cell anemia and the way that the state ignored it as a biological weapon for genoicide against Black people. Indeed, in *Body and Soul: The Black Panther Party and the Fight against Medical Discrimination*, author Alondra Nelson even argues that sickle cell anemia traits are a reaction from an awakened cellular response as a result of being forcibly removed from Africa.[40] She

40 Alondra Nelson, *Body and Soul: The Black Panther Party and the Fight against Medical Discrimination* (University of Minnesota Press, 2013).

claims that the body experiences a harsh, visceral response to relocations to North America, where Black people were forcibly brought as slaves, starting in 1525. But sickle cell is more common in Africa than in the United States, so this conspiracy theory likely has more to do with Black people's understandable fear of the U.S. government than biology. After slavery was tolerated for more than three hundred years in North America,[41] many Black people feared that the state was more intent on eradicating Black folks than eradicating sickle cell anemia. Reverberations from the Tuskegee Syphilis Experiment left many Black people distrustful of medicine.

Similarly, Black people's distrust of medicine would be reconfirmed in 1975 when the public learned about Henrietta Lacks, a Black woman in Baltimore whose cancer cells had been harvested for medical study without her knowledge or consent. In 1951, Lacks's cancer cells had been extracted because they reproduced quickly and indefinitely, staying alive long enough for greater examination. The hospital profited greatly from these findings, yet Lacks's family had not been compensated for their use. The case created further concern about privacy and the rights of Black people in medical care. Her family only found out about the harvest of Lacks's cells when the hospital began requesting more cells from each of her children 24 years later. Gradually, the children began talking to each other about these phone calls, wondering what was going on. Their fears were confirmed when Rebecca Skloot, a white reporter, dug into the case. The hospital argued that harvesting these cells for profit and

---

41 For more on the incredible story of Black people fighting for liberation during the U.S. Civil War, check out *Robert Smalls: The Slave Who Stole a Confederate Ship, Broke the Code, & Freed a Village*

without consent or knowledge was legal. The public began asking if doing so was ethical. The matter wasn't settled until 2013, when two of Lacks's grandchildren began to oversee use of the cells and could establish privacy. In 2021, the grandchildren filed a lawsuit against Thermo Fisher Scientific for profiting from Lacks's cells without consent. The disputes over use of these cells remain ongoing.

Cases like these suggest that there are similar events that we are, as of yet, unaware of. Worse, this dark history, lack of options, poor-quality services, and living as an oppressed population in an occupied country, led many Black people to avoid healthcare altogether. They viewed the hospital as a place where Black people go to die. Because of this, Sandra Ford's primary job at the clinic was to make it comfortable, approachable, and safe. She needed to dispel these fears, show that Black people could be supported and comfortable in a medical environment, and that doing so would ultimately result in better health.

For this reason, much of the Panthers strategy was to be friendly and welcoming, especially for new people. In their clinics, where anyone was welcome, Sandra Ford went out of her way to greet regulars and make new people feel like they belonged, playing popular music and carrying a chipper attitude even as people were receiving life-saving healthcare. A simple stenciled sign in the window could let you know that the clinic had radical associations but patients were not preached at with propaganda; they were cared for.

Portland's Black Panthers were also the first chapter with a dental clinic. The Malcolm X People's Dental Clinic was located on Williams Avenue and Sacramento Street, established with white advocates and allies who came to the Panthers' aid again. But still, the dental clinic was the most difficult of their endeavors. Obtaining usable equipment and volunteers was more tiresome. Lacking adequate staffing, Sandra Ford did all of the scheduling and finances for both clinics for years. While many people believed in their mission, the needs were incredibly demanding. To Sandra Ford, it strangely felt more complicated to convince trained dentists and hygienists to volunteer than to convince doctors to help at their clinic.

In July 1969, the Portland Panthers traveled to Oakland to attend The United Front Against Fascism conference where actual Black Panthers were impressed by the Portland NCCF's ability to sustain a Black organization in a city known for its lack of racial diversity. No Black Panther chapter had a dental clinic, but Portland did. With Eldridge Cleaver on the run and Huey P. Newton in prison, both their and the Black Panthers' futures were unclear. Bobby Seale attempted to maintain some sense of order in the Party. He directed resources and priorities towards the establishment of social programs and dropped the "For Self-Defense" from their name. Seale wanted to strengthen the relationship between the Black Panther Party and the communities that they served.

SKEWERED IN THE PUBLIC EYE

*I*n 1969, the FBI charged 21 members of the New York Panthers for terrorist plots in what would lead to the longest trial in state history. When they were finally put on trial thirteen months later, the jury found them innocent on all 156 charges in under an hour. It seemed like the purpose was to disrupt and distract them above anything else.

Similarly, at the 1968 Democratic National Convention (DNC), fifteen thousand protesters showed up but found themselves up against twenty thousand members of law enforcement. A few hundred protesters participated in a riot organized by the Weather Underground—a group of the Panthers' white allies who splintered from Students for a Democratic Society (SDS) when SDS refused to support the Panthers at a conference in June of 1969 because of the Panthers' sexism. Weather Underground leader Bernadine Dohrn explained "Whenever white people have a choice, you can't make that choice without thinking about how easy it is not to stand up for Black people at a given moment"[42] and half of SDS's membership followed her out the door behind the Black Panthers. Over its first few years, the Weather Underground experimented with free love and bombing police cars. They went on to bomb—with various success— the Haymarket statue in Chicago, courthouses and judges'

---

42 *Mother Country Radicals* explores the history of the Weather Underground and its connection to the Black liberation struggle. crooked.com/podcast-series/mother-country-radicals/

homes overseeing Panther trials, the National Guard building, Bank of America headquarters, and the U.S. Capitol building.

When the dust settled after the riot in Chicago, eight organizers were charged with inciting the riots—based on their prominence in the movement, not for participating—including Bobby Seale. Seale's lawyer was unavailable for the trial, so Seale asked it to be rescheduled. When that was denied, he represented himself. During the proceedings, the judge claimed Seale was in contempt and disruptive. At the judge's order, Seale was bound and gagged in the courtroom—in full view of the jury. The judge wanted Seale to be represented by one of the lawyers present and couldn't interpret Seale's insistence on representing himself as anything other than a way of disrupting the court. Seale's case is certainly the most famous incident of a defendant being bound and gagged in a courtroom, and it's nearly unbelievable. But it's happened a few times since—including in Cleveland as recently as 2018[43]—however, it has never happened in cases where the defendant was representing themselves, rendering them incapable of speech. Seale was convicted on sixteen counts of contempt and sentenced to four years.

During the trial, Seale was charged for ordering a murder in Connecticut, unrelated to the event at the DNC. George Sams was a Black Panther field marshall who traveled to New York to clean up the East Coast branch of the Party. In New York, Sams met Alex Rackley, a teenager that he then brought with him from New York to New Haven, Connecticut, and—

43 Collman, Ashley. "A Judge Ordered a Convicted Robber's Mouth Taped over in Court for Ignoring Repeated Orders to 'Zip It'." *Insider*, Insider, 2 Aug. 2018, insider.com/judge-orders-convict-gagged-with-tape-for-repeated-courtroom-outbursts-2018-8.

within two days—accused him of being a police informant. Rackley was a kid and wasn't as politically sophisticated, so he didn't know the "right" answers to the Party's questions. Sams, who had long been a troublemaker and was kicked out of the Black Panthers previously, demanded that the New Haven Party leadership torture Rackley to get the truth. After a period of torture, Rackley admitted to being a spy even though it is very likely that he was not. It is widely accepted that torture merely coerces subjects into providing information, regardless of it's veracity.

Members of the New Haven Black Panther branch then killed the teen at Sams's suggestion. In a matter of days, this incident had escalated to murder. It was also mere days after Hoover demanded that the FBI field office disrupt this particular chapter. When the New Haven Panthers were arrested, Sams was not among them. He had disappeared. Yet a tape that he had recorded of the torture ended up in the hands of police. Months later, when he was found in Canada, Sams told police that Seale had ordered the murder of Rackley. Despite only contradictory evidence, following the DNC trial, Seale was implicated and extradited to Connecticut, where he faced the death penalty. It took nearly two years for the judge to dismiss the charges. Given the evidence, it seems more likely that Sams, and not Rackley, was working for COINTELPRO. Worse, it seemed like the purpose of the operation was to put Seale out of commission as the police and courts had done with Huey P. Newton years earlier. Worst of all, the incidents in New Haven revealed the weaknesses of the Party. They had national leadership but they couldn't control individual chapters from forming elaborate conspiracy theories and going rogue.

In early 1970, the Portland Panthers organized a ballot initiative for a city charter amendment[44] for neighborhood control of police in order to reduce violence. The ballot initiative would essentially put community control of the police under oversight of each neighborhood, so law enforcement would function less like an occupying army and more like a service to each neighborhood. The initiative was strongly opposed by Mayor Schrunk who called it "unconstitutional" and "illegal," it was "reluctantly approved" by the conservative city council for the Black Panthers to gather signatures for their ballot measure. While the city government hated it, the ballot initiative was far from controversial. The reform was a popular movement, supported by such mainstream organizations as City Club of Portland—who pointed out how it was long overdue after the extensive laundry list of bad behavior from the Portland Police and disproportionate violence against Black residents.

Days after a march organized to show support for the amendment, nineteen-year-old Albert Williams—who had a larceny warrant—was standing in the doorway of the NCCF office at 5:00 p.m. When police officers Stan Harmon and Ralph Larson pulled up and called to him, he refused to approach, having been previously roughed up by Harmon. In the past, neighbors reported that Harmon had entered their homes without permission or a search warrant, Harmon claiming he didn't need one. Harmon had a reputation for

44 In part, reading, "Charter amendment requires two separate police departments, one for area predominantly Black (including Albina), other for remainder of city; each administered by three paid commissioners, appointed by paid elected neighborhood councils; police commissioners fix policies, salaries city pays, discipline policemen; abolishes police civil service; requires policemen reside within employing department."

being unnecessarily physical and Larson freely threw around the N-word. Despite having a ten-year-old in custody in the back seat, the two officers got out of the car and pointed their guns at Williams. Williams, who had a history of drug use and wasn't a member of the NCCF, went inside, locked the door, and pushed his way past Joyce Radford at the front desk.

In the following minutes, the NCCF received a phone call from a local TV station asking if they had already been raided. The station heard on the police radios that they were raiding the NCCF headquarters and wanted to confirm if they should send out a news crew. Police deny this was a raid and claim to have merely been pursuing a warrant while the officers had a minor in custody. But the evidence is questionable and seems to indicate that this event was staged for the police to raid the NCCF "Black Panther" headquarters. By all accounts except that of his own parents, Williams hadn't been inside the NCCF headquarters before so it was an odd choice of buildings to duck into when he was being pursued by police.

The NCCF offered to negotiate with the police if they put down their guns. Instead, the officers called for backup and kicked open the door. Radford failed to stop Williams, who ascended four stories and mysteriously knew the location of the NCCF rifle and bullets that Radford kept for safety. Radford pleaded with Williams and assured him that they'd make sure the police didn't hurt him. The police claim that Williams shot at them while the other witnesses claim that he put the rifle down and raised his arms to surrender. Williams was shot in the abdomen and arm, leaving him in critical condition, as Harmon promptly shouted, "I finally got him!" Rather than take Williams to the hospital two blocks

Albert Williams minutes after the shooting, outside of Panther headquarters.
Photo is the property of Oregonian Publishing Co.

away or wait for an ambulance, the officers took Williams miles away, across the river to a different hospital, risking his life in the process.

The following day, two hundred people entered city hall to protest the fact that Williams was being held on $25,000 bail on charges of attempting to kill an officer. They wanted to raise public awareness before the trial and to find white allies as incensed as they were. However, another event had a greater impact on the public's perception of the police. A month later, members of the Ohio National Guard shot thirteen Kent State student protesters, killing four and wounding nine, resulting in a massive sit-in protest at Portland State— which was successfully settled with administration after four days. Yet, before the structures could be dismantled, Portland Police showed up in riot gear and began destroying property. When students tried to intervene, riot police gassed them and beat them with batons. Thirty-one people were hospitalized, one person's head cracked open. Protesters were confused and betrayed, with one officer even describing the situation as "not pretty, but the streets are clear." Media, which had previously been critical of the protests, lambasted the police for their unnecessary violence. The PPB made a statement that they would never use force against nonviolent protesters again. With this renewed critical reception of police, seven hundred protesters again marched on the courthouse for Williams's trial.

During Williams's trial, Ford's attorney pointed out that the police knew where Williams lived and that Williams had spent two weeks in the courthouse during Ford's 1969 trial. If the police wanted to arrest Williams, they'd had plenty of opportunities with less risk of violence than raiding the NCCF.

Ford wondered how Williams could have known there was a rifle in their building. Why had he been hanging out in front of their building to begin with? In a 2022 interview, Percy Hampton told me that he believes the police arranged for Albert Williams to enter the NCCF offices so that they could conduct a raid. Ford agreed, saying, "He was an operative of theirs. It's all fixed. It was a setup from the very beginning," and offered a similar conclusion in a 2010 interview with Jules Boykoff and Martha Gies, pointing out that Williams had a strong strategic advantage but did not actually shoot the officer. Since Williams somehow knew about the rifle, if it was his intention to shoot Harmon, he had more than opportunity.

After his previous larceny charge, Williams had been let out of prison early, so, as Hampton explained, working with the police to infiltrate the NCCF could have been part of his plea agreement, and similar agreements were common. Williams's family denies this. Either way, I went back and forth with it and couldn't construct reasoning that could explain the police's actions, given better options to arrest Williams at home or at the courthouse during Ford's trial. Still, Officer Harmon was cleared of any wrongdoing and Williams's case was declared a mistrial. He would be convicted of the lesser charge of assault during his second trial. The judge did admonish the officers for poor judgment in entering the NCCF headquarters with a ten-year-old in their car, but ultimately allowed them to continue business as usual.

The news of police shooting Williams in the NCCF office was distorted to "Black Panthers . . . attempted to murder a police officer." Reporting of the incident never mentioned that Williams was not a member of the NCCF, that the police had made choices that escalated the violence, nor that the NCCF were not technically Black Panthers—yet, the reports always highlighted Williams's criminal past. The police would go on to file charges against the TV station for tipping off the Panthers, claiming they "increased the chance of violence," which is ironic at best. A Black *Oregonian* reporter who participated in police ride-alongs at the time confirmed to Dr. Jeffries that the police culture was macho, violent, and racist in the '60s and '70s.

These biased headlines made it difficult to obtain widespread support for the ballot measure maintaining community control of police. NCCF efforts were diverted from their ballot measure to supporting Williams and demonstrating yet another case of police violence. Despite receiving thousands of signatures, the NCCF ultimately fell short of the twenty-five thousand signatures needed to appear on the ballot. Instead, with the help of the Black Berets, Portland's Black militant group, the Panthers began their own patrols of their neighborhoods, to protect it from police. One notable difference from other chapters is that Portland's Black Panthers were not operating armed patrols and policing the police. They were observing and sharing information, exchanging strong words. There was never an armed standoff between Portland's Black Panthers and the Portland Police. However, being smeared in the press because of the Williams incident only further led the Portland Panthers away from the signature beret and leather jacket, and towards a rejection of paramilitary rhetoric while focusing on social services and civilian oversight.

As far as motive, the police have a vested interest in preventing citizen oversight. Much like governments that have anti-sedition laws, the Portland Police have been opposed to oversight since the very beginning. In 1942, John Hayes, a former union pinball mechanic turned police officer, organized the Portland Police Association (PPA),[45] the first successful labor union for police in the United States. The union was created in response to budget reforms by Police Chief Harry Niles, with the agreement that it could not go on strike. The police union was unpopular from the start. Hayes was soon removed from the office of PPA Union President for being too young and replaced by Otto Miners, a member of the German-American Bund, a U.S. pro-Nazi organization.[46]

In 1968, the Portland City Council finally recognized the PPA as an official labor union with the right to collectively bargain. When union negotiations intensified, PPA Presidents would pull criminal files about city employees, report details about their political enemies to friends in the press, and—when they couldn't find any dirt on their enemies—they would feign as though they had amassed damning files on them. In one negotiation with the city, the PPA President placed a folder in a visible position, labeled with the name of one of the city employees. His goal was to manufacture paranoia, explaining that he enjoyed "making people feel guilty—even when they are not." When this still proved unsuccessful, the PPA went back to their union to remove

45 In the fine spirit of self-publishing, the Portland Police union tells its own story in *Pickets, Pistols, and Politics: A History of the Portland Police Association* (1996)

46 A German immigrant, Miners was a member of the Bund until it was dismantled years after World War II.

the clause that prohibited them from striking. In 1969, the police went on strike and shut down the docks, crippling the economy, forcing the City of Portland to give the police a raise. Just about every city in the United States now uses this method as a best practice for police negotiations.

In 2018, Oxford's study of the largest one hundred U.S. cities showed a direct correlation between an increase in union protections for police officers and abuse against citizens. A 2019 study from the University of Chicago found that once Florida Sheriffs' Deputies received union rights, incidents of violent police conduct increased 40 percent statewide. The more collective bargaining rights police have, the more people are killed by police, with a disproportionate number of those being Black people.

Portland Police had faced federal scrutiny for years because of unnecessary violence as well as the racketeering operation that plagued the department in the '50s. With this as the backdrop, it's not surprising that even City Club of Portland supported police reform. The NCCF ballot initiative is remarkably similar to contemporary police reforms, attempting to create community control of police. The police had a complaint board, but could easily ignore complaints. If it wasn't so painful, it would be ironic that the NCCF ballot initiative was stomped out by the police, who had left Williams, a teenager, in critical condition. The media reported that the Black Panthers were the cause of this violence, when the NCCF's involvement was entirely incidental. It would be years before similar police reforms were enacted, and mechanisms for the community to police the police remain minimal to this day.

As the Black Panthers rose up, the FBI sought to drag them back down by any means necessary. The headlines damning the Panthers made funding for the NCCF clinics much more difficult. The local effort to eradicate the NCCF clinics was simultaneous to a national FBI program to dismantle the Black Panther Party through COINTELPRO tactics—surveillance, infiltration, subversion, and co-optation.

Hoover repurposed the FBI agents who, in the '50s, had brought indictments against 115 Portland Police officers for criminal behavior, and created a coalition to work together to destroy the Portland Black Panthers. Again, the Portland Black Panthers were not a militant organization. They did not kill anyone. They did not even operate armed patrols of the police. They merely ran social service programs better than the government and were vocal in ways that were often inconvenient for the city's agenda. However, it didn't matter that the Panthers weren't committing crimes. The FBI didn't have government oversight so they could tell whatever story they wanted without being challenged.

Often, COINTELPRO worked through a series of entrapments. For example, in 2003, a kid in his mid-twenties walked into Microcosm's office and began with, "Hey, I'm looking for some people that want to blow up a gas station." Which is a strange introduction but when someone asked, "Why?" he says, "You know, mess things up. Power to the people." I don't know for sure that this kid was a COINTELPRO plant, but I never saw him again and his tactics made no sense. They don't build anything. There is no crescendo. They aren't strategic. They wreak of entrapment and are part and parcel of how the FBI conducts itself.

The FBI then takes anyone with interest—even people who go along with a plan out of social and relational obligations to help someone who they think is their "friend"— and prosecute them as though they were the leader. In many well-publicized cases, the sole instigator of terrorism is the FBI agent.[47] The FBI and local police used these same tactics to attempt to infiltrate the Portland NCCF and to push them to mindless violence.

In a strange example, the FBI designed and distributed coloring books showing Black people committing violent acts against whites, purportedly mailed to white liberals by the Black Panthers. By distorting the Panther ideology in this manner with pointlessly violent content, the FBI believed that they could eliminate Panther funding. With no funding, it would then be easy to criminalize the group and discredit them—even if the line never traced back to the Panthers.

Another tactic is "snitch-jacketing," making it falsely appear like a member is an undercover government operative. The other members become suspicious and the organization is divided into factions. One of the most noteworthy incidents of this within the Black Panthers was Stokely Carmichael. After Carmichael appeared on *Face the Nation* in 1966, saying that Black people shouldn't fight in Vietnam, President Lyndon Johnson requested that the FBI snitch-jacket Carmichael in 1968:[48]

47 Mora, Nicolás Medina, and Mike Hayes. "Did the FBI Transform This Teenager into a Terrorist after Reading His Emails?" *BuzzFeed News*, BuzzFeed News, 16 Nov. 2015, buzzfeednews.com/article/nicolasmedinamora/did-the-fbi-transform-this-teenager-into-a-terrorist.
48 *The COINTELPRO Papers*, Ward Churchill, South End Press, 2001

> . . . consideration be given to convey the impression
> that CARMICHAEL is a CIA informer. One method
> of accomplishing would be to have a carbon copy
> of an informant report supposedly written by
> CARMICHAEL to the CIA carefully deposited in the
> automobile of a close Black Nationalist friend . . .

This trick was entirely too successful. Huey P. Newton was made aware of the forged memo and revoked Carmichael's Party membership. Factions formed and paranoia ensued. Nobody knew who was an informant, who was made to look like an informant, and who was loyal to the Party. Who could you trust? The fact that Fred Hampton's close friend had been successfully bribed to murder him did not help matters. Rumors abounded. Quickly, there were major disputes between East Coast and West Coast branches of the Black Panther Party. Like the George Sams and Alex Rackley incident, members of the Party were tortured and some were killed for fear that they were government rats. Remember, in the most famous case of George Sams, it seemed more likely that the murderer was an informant rather than the murderee. It was everything that the FBI could have hoped for. These cases are useful in understanding how the FBI targeted Portland, similarly.

A wedge was effectively driven between Huey P. Newton and Eldridge Cleaver in the national leadership. From Algeria, Eldridge was still directing forces loyal to him in Oakland. When the driver of a *Black Panther* newspaper truck robbed a gas station, Newton attempted to lay down a strict code of conduct for Black Panthers while Cleaver called for violent revolution. Members could be kicked out, in attempts to remove COINTELPRO infiltrators and members who had acted against the group's values. But Cleaver and Newton—the two people ousting members—were themselves both loose cannons. Cleaver was accused of calling out a murder on Sam Napier for being a Newton loyalist. Newton was accused of calling out a murder on Robert Webb for being a Cleaver loyalist.[49] Many murders of Black Panthers during the next few years remain unsolved. In some cities, Black Panthers were simply murdered by police and then ther murders were rationalized by a public campaign to make them appear justified and necessary.

Throughout this period, the Portland Panthers didn't take sides and continued to run their social service programs. They were widely known in the Black community as the people that you approach when you have a problem. Which is much better than being known as the people who can't get along with each other and are being torn apart by their own drama.

The Portland NCCF believed that the local police had a hand in influencing reports in the *Oregonian*, but that was nothing compared to what the FBI did nationally with the media. Hoover's racism underpinned much of his cognitive distortions. He assumed that anyone who was his political enemy was inferior and thus befitting of the lies that he propagated about them, just as he believed Black people were inferior to him. It seems that the Black Panther Party offended Hoover so much because it defied both his view of Black people as inferior and his belief that they should stay in

49 "4 PANTHERS ADMIT GUILT IN SLAYING," *New York Times,* nytimes. com/1973/05/22/archives/4-panthers-admit-guilt-in-slaying-plead-to-a-reduced-charge-of.html

their place. The FBI justified their efforts to mislead the public because no matter how treacherous, heavy handed, and quasi-legal police behavior became, Hoover felt it was necessary to dismantle the Black Panther Party as a matter of public safety. Indeed, these were the same tactics that Hoover had used to end Dr. King's civil rights movement.[50]

All over the United States, newspapers began running incendiary headlines about the destructive nature of the Black Panther Party. Any crime involving Black participants—protagonists or victims—would be pinned on the Black Panther Party, even with little or no connection. Police departments would conduct raids of Black Panther headquarters and manufacture situations that would result in shoot-outs—all to prove that the Panthers were so ruthless that they must be stopped at any cost. Otherwise, they risked the Panthers corrupting their children with free food and healthcare.

In Portland, the tactics were similarly diabolical: police constantly arrested as many "Black Panthers" as possible, prevented people from getting involved in the organization, cut off all lines of support from allies, and sowed seeds of suspicion amongst the members of the NCCF until they were pointing fingers at each other. FBI agents would constantly surveil NCCF headquarters and homes, going door-to-door to spread false information about members to their neighbors, coworkers, parents, employers, and community. The House of Sound record store suffered multiple FBI raids solely on the grounds that the owner was friends with Ford and gave money to the clinics. Suited agents would approach

---

50 Check out my book, *The CIA Makes Science Fiction Unexciting: Dark Deeds & Derring-Do* for the whole story.

people with proximity to a party member and ask, "Do you know that so-and-so is involved with the Black Panther Party? We need to turn them around in the right direction." This was often the most effective way of extracting information from concerned parties and some people approached in this manner did become informants.

Portland NCCF members would be followed everywhere they went. The FBI approached them, partially to seek informants and partially to convince other members that another member was already an informant. Recovered Portland Police surveillance files are mostly incoherent, trying to connect dots and show that people were terrorists, despite no criminal record. The FBI sent letters to Portland NCCF volunteers to convince them to quit providing medical resources at the clinics. They urged Multnomah County to create "competing" free clinics outside of the Panther moniker. The FBI publicly criticized the Portland NCCF on the grounds that the bulk of their healthcare volunteers and doctors were white. Ironically, Black healthcare providers and doctors were afraid to become involved with the Black Panther Party or even Dr. King's civil rights movement because of the risks of becoming FBI targets. Consequently, the most vocal supporters and people who showed up for Black Panther rallies in Portland were white. One doctor, when questioned about choosing to be involved despite the risks of being on an FBI list, responded, "God has a list too."

These tactics were effective because they drove Black Panther support underground. The Portland NCCF was incredibly effective at spreading information through more traditional means but they could not dream of comparing their resources to the FBI, who could effectively shame their supporters and bolster their critics, harassing everyone who offered so much as moral encouragement publicly. This transformed public support into quiet conversations among trusted company.

February 14, 1970, Police surveillance photos, Courtesy of Portland City Archives, A2004-005.2959 : Black Panthers demonstration in support of "repressed peoples." U.S Courthouse. L-R, Kent Ford, Freddie Whitlow, and Percy Hampton

PAYING FOR IT

*A*fter three years, the "Free Huey" campaign, led by Assata Shakur,[51] was successful and Huey P. Newton was released in 1970. There were problems with the evidence in his first trial and subsequent mistrials. Newton was defended by an Armenian communist lawyer, who had obtained his law license without going to college. Newton's lawyer defended him on political grounds because he believed in the importance of these social movements. Other Panther chapters began taking notes about their own defense strategies in court—but none were as successful as Ford's defense and civil suit. Still, Newton had spent three years in prison—most of the life of the Party—but beating the charges was a huge triumph for activists around the world.

When Ford returned to Oakland and lifted weights with Newton that summer, most people assumed that he was already a Black Panther. Newton's time in prison had significantly changed how he viewed politics and the future of the Black Panthers. He wanted to reinvent the Party as social servants, ensuring survival for daily needs. Newton described the "survival programs" thusly:[52]

> All these programs satisfy the deep needs of the community but they are not solutions to our problems. That is why we call them survival

---

51 An extensive campaign continued against her godson, Tupac Shakur, which is detailed by John Potash in *The FBI War on Tupac Shakur: State Repression of Black Leaders from the Civil Rights Era to the 1990s*

52 *Survival Pending Revolution: What the Black Panthers Can Teach the U.S. Food Movement* ...https://archive.foodfirst.org/wp-content/uploads/2013/12/BK18_2-2012_Summer_Survival_Pending_Revolution.pdf.

programs, meaning survival pending revolution. We say that the survival program of the Black Panther Party is like the survival kit of a sailor stranded on a raft. It helps him to sustain himself until he can get completely out of that situation. So the survival programs are not answers or solutions, but they will help us to organize the community around a true analysis and understanding of their situation.

The logic was that with their basic needs met, Black people would be more equipped to organize the revolution. These were the exact services that Portland NCCF had honed in on from the start: clothing the poor, feeding the hungry, escorting people in danger, educating the oppressed, and healing the sick. Ford and Newton got to talking and Newton considered Portland for full membership as a Black Panther Party chapter. Newton asked Ford how many buildings they had. Ford responded "Three, including a dental clinic." No other chapter had a dental clinic and many groups were struggling with the mandate to switch from acquiring guns to serving free breakfast to children and setting up health clinics. Newton was impressed with the Portland NCCF's convictions and achievements. By the late summer of 1970, the NCCF received a letter from Oakland saying that they were officially a chapter of the Black Panther Party. According to Floyd Cruse and other members of the party, Ford was made the leader on account of his willingness to listen, ability to make decisions cerebrally, to see plans through, and take responsibility for outcomes.

Perhaps because they were not a formal Black Panther Party, or simply because they rejected the formality, the

Portland Black Panthers did not use the traditional roles as established by the national Black Panther Party. Typically, the leader of the chapter is the "Minister of Defense" or "Deputy Chairman," but Ford simply took the title of "captain." Most chapters had a Minister of Information, whereas Portland chose Floyd Cruse to be the deputy minister of information— even though Oscar Johnson, assistant deputy minister of education, researched and wrote Cruse's speeches. Tom Venters became deputy minister of education. Raymond Joe was deputy chief of staff and Percy Hampton was in charge of newspaper distribution. Many of the central members such as Sandra Ford and Linda Thornton didn't hold leadership positions, but managed the clinics and donations, respectively. Portland did have a deputy minister of defense in Tommy Mills, who had returned from Vietnam as a decorated war hero praised by Oregon's governor, and became second in command, training the group on weapons operation, counterinsurgency, and security. Oscar Johnson had also served in the Marine Corps, and brought those skills the group. In Kent Ford's infinite humbleness, he often only refers to himself as the "co-founder of the Portland chapter."

Unlike chapters in other cities, according to the members, the Portland branch was not built on chauvinism and patriarchy. Nationally, the Black Panthers were about 60 percent women but few held leadership positions despite notable exceptions like Elaine Brown.[53] Since many members

53 Elaine Brown became the chair of the entire Black Panther Party in 1974, though Field Marshall Donald Cox insists that this was the day that the Black Panther Party ceased to exist. Geronimo Pratt claimed that Brown was, in fact, an FBI infiltrator. Pratt claims that Brown came to lead the Party by locking her boyfriend, Huey P. Newton, in a house with women and cocaine after he got out of prison, until he was addicted and neutralized for the rest of his life. Pratt spent 27 years in prison before

joined in high school or college, the organization was remarkably young. In Oakland, the Black Panther Party had a deep history of sexism,[54] with Eldridge Cleaver describing women as being involved in the movement only to have sex with and suggesting that women's power was withholding sex for political reasons.[55] When asked about women's position in the movement, Black Panther Jewel Cook answered "prone."[56] In many chapters, women were only allowed to assume leadership positions when critical amounts of men were imprisoned or attacked by police, whereas the power structure in the Portland chapter was much more equal on grounds of gender. Women ran the programs and answered to no one. This is partially because Portland organized much less formal roles and partially because the power structure was more balanced. Sexist behavior was quickly dispelled and the women advocated for themselves and each other. Despite what was happening to the Party nationally and in the press,

---

his own conviction was overturned. Evidence had been hidden from the jury that showed Pratt's innocence, including a receipt signed by Elaine Brown from the paint shop that had repainted Pratt's car to match the car involved in the crime. FBI Agent M. Wesley Swearingen corroborated how odd it was that Elaine Brown's FBI file was empty, which is almost always an indication of information that has been redacted for being sensitive. It's important to note that the leader of the Party was thought by a significant percentage of the membership to be working for the FBI. Everything about the Party became divisive.

54 "Women in the Black Panther Party, A roundtable" Ashley Farmer, Mary Phillips, Robyn C. Spencer and Leela Yellesetty isreview.org/issue/111/women-black-panther-party/index.html

55 "A Woman's Place in the Revolution: Gender and Sexual Politics within the Black Panther Party," Anna Freyberga pubs.lib.umn.edu/index.php/muraj/article/download/3367/2790/18590

56 *Mother Country Radicals* explores the history of the Weather Underground and its connection to the Black liberation struggle. crooked.com/podcast-series/mother-country-radicals/

the future of the newly formalized Portland Black Panther chapter looked bright.

Still, to operate all of these programs, the Black Panthers needed money. They handled most of their fundraising through selling the Party newspaper. This responsibility was handled by Percy Hampton, who sold papers one at a time for a quarter, sending half of the money back to Oakland. When I asked Hampton why this job interested him, he responded the same way that Cruse had when I asked him why he joined the Party, "They picked the job for me. I didn't have a choice. They wanted me to be the distribution manager. To get into

Police surveillance photo of Linda Thornton

the Party, you had to go out there and sell papers and they needed someone to coordinate that."

The Portland Panthers went from distributing three hundred to eight hundred copies each week—everywhere from college campuses to grocery stores to liquor stores. However, the paper would serve a much more important purpose than fundraising.

In 1970, the state of Oregon organized Vortex I: A Biodegradable Festival of Life concert, featuring loads of peacenik bands from the region along with dancing and drugs. The event was organized solely for the purpose of pausing anti-war protests by sending radicals thirty miles out of town during an American Legion national convention.[57] If a government-sponsored event encouraging as many as one hundred thousand peaceniks[58] to engage in sanctioned illegal drug use, naked dancing, and hippie music during an era of intense government surveillance isn't weird enough, consider the timing. Months prior, the Rolling Stones organized the Altamont Festival[59] fifty miles east of Oakland to bring Woodstock to the West Coast. Most notably, Altamont ended in complete disaster, with security guards[60] stabbing a gun-brandishing attendee to death twenty feet from the front of the stage[61] as the (allegedly unaware) Rolling Stones kicked

---

57 "Vortex 1: How a Rock Festival Saved Portland from Chaos." *Opb*, opb. org/video/2020/08/28/vortex-1-how-a-rock-festival-saved-portland-from-chaos/.

58 Official estimates range as widely as 30,000–100,000 attendees.

59 Featuring Santana; Jefferson Airplane; Crosby, Stills, Nash & Young; and the Grateful Dead, a veritable who's who of the era.

60 Security comprised dozens of Hells Angels members paid with beer, in order to not involve police officers.

61 Captured on film in *Gimme Shelter* (1970), with a pivotal scene of Mick

into "Under My Thumb." Three other audience members died through various accidents and four live births somehow also occurred during the concert. After hearing that "security" had knocked the singer of Jefferson Airplane unconscious during their performance, the Grateful Dead opted not to perform. For many, the disastrous event signified and marked a tumultuous end to the '60s, seemingly showing that hippies didn't necessarily have better answers to the United States's cultural problems than anyone else. For the state of Oregon, it was advantageous to recreate a similar event.

Weeks before reelection, Republican Governor Tom McCall decided that this recreation was apparently the best solution to preventing violent clashes by separating the anti-war movement from the pro-war movement. In order to entice tens of thousands to the governor's party, law enforcement was suspended at Vortex I. The story is almost unbelievable, and what strikes me is how the government condoned criminality for white attendees at the concert while simultaneously cracking down on Black Portland residents for committing no crimes. Nonetheless, the Black Panthers identified a strategic opportunity. To the Black Panthers, Vortex I was a great place to sell newspapers. Sent on assignment by the Party, Percy Hampton showed up with Panther member Willy James Brown and a car full of *Black Panther* newspapers. They began selling them as they walked towards the entrance.

In a 2022 interview, Hampton extols the event, saying, "It was a big ole hippie fest over Labor Day weekend. Everyone was high and getting drunk. Dancing naked. It was a big party.

Jagger watching the footage in the editing room.

There wasn't a cop in sight." When the crowd began building a stage out of scrap lumber from collapsed barns, a helicopter appeared out of nowhere. After landing, several men in suits emerged and asked the peaceniks what they needed to build a proper stage. The next day, heavy equipment and new douglas fir beams were inexplicably delivered. During the concert, when a speaker from the stage directed people to where they could get help if they were having a bad trip, the speaker was booed for "being negative." Just like the Black Panthers, everyone at Vortex I was fed for free. And just like the Black Panthers, the government carefully surveilled every detail and aspect of Vortex I from a secret hotel room—with a SWAT team carefully hidden in a park maintenance building onsite.

The peaceniks at Vortex I loved the *Black Panther* papers— Hampton and Brown ran out of copies of the new issue, as well as every back issue, just while walking towards the entrance. They sold every copy in Hampton's car and came back the next day with more. When I asked Hampton if there was anything odd, he replied, "Well, there [were] no police . . . we expected a lot more resistance." I pressed Hampton for accounts of the most extreme portraits from the event. The most that he would offer is that it was too wild for him to spend the night camping at the park so he went home and returned in the morning. Vortex I clearly wasn't the kind of environment where Hampton was comfortable. However, it also felt like I had bumped into an unspoken rule: he didn't want to divulge other people's illegal behavior to a reporter, even when it was government sanctioned and fifty years later. In addition to demonstrating how the state treats Black and white people differently, Vortex I is important because it showed that the Portland Black Panther Party had a strong group of white supporters who were willing to fund their revolution. The paper was a way for the Panthers to achieve both outreach and financial support from white leftists who believed in what they were doing but weren't comfortable working directly in their clinics.

Those white, anti-war hippies couldn't get enough copies of the *Black Panther* newspaper. The paper was engrossing, relevant, far left, and contained local news from each chapter, alongside national and international news. White radicals liked the *Black Panther* newspaper because it was difficult to find newspapers and magazines that spoke from their point of view. Other Black newspapers embraced capitalism and colonialism, often working from the perspective of aging and increasingly conservative executives. The Black Panthers had a similar ideology to other '60s radicals—and in fact could help inform and educate them.

Any financial needs unmet by newspaper sales were supplemented with private donations from local businesses and individuals, weekly or monthly. However, the *Oregonian* framed these requests as extortive. In one article, the *Oregonian* reported that the Black Panthers would have six members wait outside while Portland Panther fundraiser Linda Thornton would go inside and talk to the manager, with the implication that violence would result if the businesses did not donate. In reality, this fear seems rooted in racism[62] and neither the *Oregonian* nor the FBI could find accounts of these "shakedowns," though Ford admits to Dr. Jeffries that "Tommy Mills, a serious, no-nonsense guy [who

62 Statistically, most violent crime is carried out by white men against white men.

was a physically intimidating and a decorated Vietnam war veteran] 'might have been too assertive' when inquiring about donations," adding "On these occasions, I would be sure to ask Tommy to tone it down." In FBI memos about meeting with donors to the Portland programs, the agents noted that donors described the Panthers as pleasant to work with and that Thornton would routinely remind supporters that they don't need money for breakfast programs during the summer. The FBI noted that the NCCF didn't take money when they didn't need it. In fact, the Panthers chose Thornton *because* she was of unimposing stature as well as pleasant and polite. They were well aware of the fear and perception of Black people, so they thought it would be difficult for people to misconstrue her as a threat.

As Kent Ford explained on KBOO, "Anything that you say to these guys, they get something out of it, whether you think they did or not." Percy Hampton cuts in, "They are fishing for information. If they can get enough on any of us, they are going to destroy our lives." Panther researcher and speechwriter Oscar Johnson finished the thought, "I was working for the phone company and they were trying to get me fired. They asked me to lunch a couple of times to get information. They were parked in front of my house for six days a week. I was talking to a friend at work about this and he told me that, 'You are crazy,' so one day coming from school, I knocked on the FBI's car window and asked them, 'Hey, you guys want anything?' They drove off and my friend said, 'You were right!' and we weren't even doing anything!"

Ford told me that in 1986 he received a phone call from journalist Bill Keller, who had been a reporter at the

Oregonian in 1971 before moving on to the *Washington Post* and the *New York Times*. While the vast majority of *Oregonian* coverage merely painted the Panthers as one-dimensional cartoon villains—loosely attempting to associate them with any crime or violence—the membership could tell that this time it was different. Keller had done some reporting on the Portland Black Panthers and Ford recalls, with a strong tenor of emotion in his voice, that their 1971 interview was so pleasant that he did not "want the tape to end." The two had formed a bond, and in 1986, Keller got back in touch. The FBI had dumped a number of files concerning the Panthers and Keller wanted to relate the findings to Ford. And they were juicy. Keller told Ford about an FBI plot for the Panthers to offer fruit at the breakfast program for kids to take to school. The FBI would intervene at the source and inject laxatives into the fruit before it was delivered to the breakfast program. The idea was that the kids would take the fruit to school, get sick, and—the FBI believed—make the decision to stop attending the breakfast program. Poisoning children is *almost* too evil of a plot even for the FBI, and the story was hard to believe. I reached out to Keller, but at 73 he's no longer giving interviews, citing his memory. Few people in their 70s are as sharp as Kent Ford. However, I did find numerous corroborating sources about this story, including the FBI's own files.[63] It's impossible to know if the FBI ever attempted this plot in Portland, as those details are not disclosed, but the mere proposal is plenty horrific all its own and the FBI files disclose that agents were rewarded most for concocting horrific schemes to undermine public trust in the Panthers.

---

63 *The COINTELPRO Papers*, Ward Churchill, South End Press, 2001

The Black Panther Party was attempting to create permanent solutions to century-old problems. Thornton would more likely mention funding their clinics instead of mentioning the Black Panthers, due to the public campaign to cast Black Panthers as violent. The *Oregonian* claimed that the Black Panthers would phone in bomb threats to businesses that didn't donate to them—despite having no proof of this.[64] When I asked Ford about this, he explained that they wanted peaceable relationships with these donors. They were unarmed and nonviolent. Further, it didn't make sense to them to threaten a business, knowing that they would be returning a month later to ask for donations for their clinics.

The Portland Police followed up on the *Oregonian*'s tip and began interrogating businesses, looking into whether their donations were given willfully or extorted. They even went so far as to urge businesses *not* to support the Black Panthers. Next, the police fed a tip to the *Oregonian*, who reported on the Panthers soliciting donations without a permit. The article states that numerous permit applications were delivered and mailed to the Black Panther office but none were registered. In reality, the Black Panthers did apply for a permit through the appropriate channels. City code allows council to deny permits to those who "were not a responsible person of good character and reputation . . . and [thus] control and the supervision of the solicitation will not be under a responsible and reliable person." To this point, numerous Black and white character witnesses testified for ninety minutes at Portland

64 Jules Boykoff, and Martha Gies. "'We're Going to Defend Ourselves': The Portland Chapter of the Black Panther Party and the Local Media Response." *Oregon Historical Quarterly*, vol. 111, no. 3, 2010, pp. 278–311. *JSTOR*, https://doi.org/10.5403/oregonhistq.111.3.0278. Accessed 24 May 2022.

City Hall in favor of the Black Panthers receiving a solicitation permit. In opposition, a sole white police officer merely stated that he was present and offered no testimony. The motion for a solicitation permit was denied with no explanation offered, because, clearly, none was needed. In response to the situation, even the usually hostile *Oregonian* published an op-ed in support of the permit, stating that the programs the Black Panthers offered were the "first time their youngsters had breakfast or the first time they were able to get a tooth pulled without feeling like they were the scum of the earth." The solicitation permit wasn't granted until a large public outcry forced the city's hand.

When the resistance to the solicitation permit didn't work to stop the Portland Black Panthers' efforts, the Portland Police increased their public misinformation campaign against the Panthers. The police confused or conflated the Black Panthers with the Nation of Islam and began distributing a *New York Times* article about anti-Zionism to Jewish community leaders in Portland. Perhaps in the police's mind, all Black community groups were the same?

In the early '70s, William Davis became the director of the clinical research medical lab at Legacy Emanuel Medical Center. Davis, who was Black, had condemned the state of Oregon for neglect and an epidemic attack on Black folks in the form of sickle cell anemia. In return for volunteering to help the Black Panthers with their own clinic, Davis was visited in his home by an FBI agent and the FBI began a line of questions meant to intimidate him. But the most curious aspect was that the FBI had clearly gotten some bad information. They interrogated Williams Davis about the presumption that he was going to replace Kent Ford as the leader of the Black Panther Party. Who gave them this impression? We will likely never know.

Police Surveillance Photos, February 14, 1970, Courtesy of Portland City Archives, A2004-005.2960 : Black Panthers demonstration in support of "repressed peoples." U.S Courthouse. "Bob" and Linda Thornton.

TO PROTECT AND SERVE

When stories of Black kids being harassed and beaten on their way home from school by students and faculty began circulating, the Panthers organized an escort to walk them home safely. It was a move reminiscent of the National Guard doing the same thing in Arkansas fourteen years earlier. Even when gangs of white people swelled to confront the escorts, the Panthers were steady. When violence happened at the school and hate speech was shouted at the students, the Panthers organized the students to boycott the school until the administration would take action. The President of Portland State University authorized use of a satellite building run by Albina resident Harold Williams for the protesting students to continue learning while a local restaurant owner served the students lunch. After two weeks, the superintendent of Portland Public Schools invited the students and their parents to a retreat and resolved the problem. The boycott was a success.

During a 2022 walking tour, I asked Ford about Harold Williams, who had previously operated a neighborhood financial consultancy out of what are now Microcosm's offices, and Ford responded "Harold had a good heart, always for the people, but sometimes misguided." While diplomatic, this portrait is revealing. For many residents of Albina growing up during the '60s and '70s, there was a lack of reasonable options towards upward mobility. The urge towards selfishness was often tempting, and while these circumstances don't justify blue- or white-collar crime, they help us to understand it in context.

In Spring of 1970, after some Black men had been mugging white patrons leaving a pool hall, Ford organized a meeting to confront the thieves. Ford stressed that, while it might feel like the only way to become upwardly mobile, it would ultimately only attract a larger police presence that could threaten their clinic and social services. By robbing white patrons, the thieves were making life more difficult for all Black people in Portland. The message resonated and in these moments the Panthers were once again effective in providing a better model for policing their own neighborhoods, one of outreach rather than persecution.

In the course of his usual duties, Ford gave a tour of the Panthers' clinics to Irving "Al" Laviske, the owner of six local McDonald's locations, including the one in Albina. Ford was hopeful that Laviske would donate to their programs, and felt that the meeting went well—though their time together was largely uneventful. Laviske responded to the tour by giving a televised interview, claiming that the Black Panthers were extorting him. Laviske claimed that he had offered to donate food, but the Panthers demanded money. Ford was bewildered. They had never discussed specifics of what donations might look like. Ford couldn't figure out how this had happened after such a positive meeting, and was shocked at Laviske's dishonesty.

This conflict is covered extensively by Dr. Jeffries in *The Portland Black Panthers*, but he never reaches the key detail. Due to freedom of information requests, we now know that the meeting was a ruse and Laviske had begun working with the police and FBI, who had long maintained that Portland Panthers extorted businesses, yet had identified zero instances. It seems that Laviske had been recruited to "prove" the story that the FBI wanted to tell Portland. These charges were then printed in the newspapers without being fact-checked. Unbeknownst to Ford, all of his phone calls with Laviske were being recorded and turned over to police.

Al Laviske attempted to file a restraining order against Ford but even with the recorded phone calls, there was no evidence of extortion. When police and FBI agents contacted other local businesses to corroborate the extortion allegations, donors exclusively gave positive accounts of their relationship with the Black Panthers. Nonetheless, media reporting continued to push the narrative that the Black Panthers were extorting local businesses. Shocked and confused, the Panthers established boycotts of the McDonald's, with the goal of disrupting business and forcing the media to acknowledge the real story. After some research, Ford discovered that Black employees at McDonald's had a low glass ceiling, almost never being promoted above entry-level jobs. While Ford acknowledges that this was merely a tactical ruse to provide leverage for McDonald's to fund them, the Black Panthers pointed to McDonald's record profits in 1970 during their simultaneous refusal to support the Black community. The Panthers argued that McDonald's had the cash in their pockets, so why weren't they supporting community organizing in their own neighborhood?

For one month, the Panthers picketed in front of McDonald's for eight hours on weekdays and ten hours on weekends. Finally, after Laviske claimed they were making threats and destroying his property, a judge issued an injunction to cease the picket. Undeterred, the Panthers kept picketing, and a week later, they were summoned to trial. Unfortunately for McDonald's, a 1968 U.S. Supreme Court case ruled that pickets are protected free speech and cannot be injuncted without a public hearing. Despite the Panthers' four attorneys, after hearing charges and countercharges, the judge limited the picket to ten Panthers who could distribute information on the premises for the next year.

One week later, a stick of dynamite detonated in front of the McDonald's—shattering its front window. No Black Panthers were ever connected to this explosion, but in the mind of the media, the blast was intrinsically tied to the Panthers' picketing. The same year, a Portland Police community relations office was bombed, as was Portland City Hall[65] and quite a few other targets all over the United States—many of them apparently the work of FBI agent provocateurs.[66] The Panthers denied anything to do with the McDonald's explosion, correctly pointing out that their efforts were already effective and they were cooperating with the judge's ruling. They explained that they had nothing to gain by setting off an explosion.

But then the most confusing development occurred. For whatever reason, the McDonald's manager relented. Laviske summoned Ford to meet with him and began the meeting by refusing to donate to the Panthers. As Ford got up to leave, the manager then offered fifty pounds of meat and five hundred

---

65 Resulting in two FBI agents showing up that same morning at Kent and Sandra Ford's home, who didn't yet know of the bombing. The crime remains unsolved.

66 *The COINTELPRO Papers*, Ward Churchill, South End Press, 2001

disposable cups per week to the Black Panther breakfast program—the same offer that Laviske claimed he made in the media after their first meeting. Within another year, their relationship had dramatically improved. The Panthers had permission to use the same McDonald's parking lot for sickle cell anemia testing. As an incentive for Black people to get tested, McDonald's even offered a coupon for a free meal. Since Kent Ford had moved to Portland, Laviske had let the police congregate and transfer suspects in the McDonald's parking lot. At the request of the Black Panthers, McDonald's stopped letting police officers use their parking lot like a police substation. While this location had warmed, the principal problems at the corporate level remain unresolved to this day. As recently as 2020, 52 Black McDonald's franchise managers sued the parent company for patterns of discrimination and undisclosed costs for franchisers, blocking them from ideal locations.[67]

Police and FBI documents offer no further explanation as to Laviske's motives or his complete turnaround regarding the Black Panthers. When I asked Ford, he had no answers for the change of heart either and did not know that Laviske was working for the FBI. He said, "I'm not surprised. It makes sense. I approached him in good faith and then he's on TV calling us a bunch of extortionists. We couldn't get away from that [rumor]. We thought the phone was being tapped and considered sending our phone bill for the police to pay each month."Then it occurred to me. The lack of exposition

67 "How McDonald's Made Enemies of Black Franchisees," Bloomberg, Susan Berfield, bloomberg.com/news/features/2021-12-17/black-mcdonald-s-franchise-owners-face-off-with-fast-food-restaurant-over-racism

and documentation could explain Laviske's sudden change of behavior. Why didn't the police or FBI question the Black Panthers regarding the bombing of McDonald's when they did regarding the bombing of city hall? Could it be because they already knew the answer? Why would such a violent and dangerous escalation make Laviske stop working with the police and start working with the Panthers? Why do the police and FBI files not focus on the explosion after focusing so intensely on manufacturing a hostile relationship between McDonald's and the Black Panthers for the previous year? Was Al Laviske's confusing turnaround a result of what he saw and learned about how far the FBI will go to escalate a conflict? Unfortunately, we will never know because he took this information to the grave many years ago.

Soon after the conflict settled with Laviske, Charles James, a Black man, requested leave from his duties in the U.S. Navy to remain at home with his pregnant fiancée. For unclear reasons, his request was not processed and instead, four plain-clothed FBI agents soon appeared at his home to retrieve him and, while the un-uniformed invaders were putting on the handcuffs, the family's German shepherd escaped the clutches of his young brother, leaping on an agent. The agents responded by choking the young brother—whose eyes bulged out as he faced turned blue—which invoked the wrath of his seventeen-year-old sister, Cheryl James, who began beating the agents with a rolling pin, demanding that her brother be released from the deadly choke hold. Charles was arrested and within the hour, the FBI returned for his spirited sister—with a dozen agents in tow—but accidentally arrested the *wrong sister*, Martha. Both Cheryl and Martha were imprisoned in an adult facility, though Martha was released shortly.

At the recommendation of a community leader, Kent Ford got in touch with the family to offer support. Quickly, a coalition was formed to bail Cheryl James out of jail so that the honor roll student could finish high school and to spread public awareness about her situation. The prosecution used one agent's badly bloodstained shirt as evidence and James was denied a jury and sentenced to eighteen months in prison for defending her brother from being murdered with a rolling pin. She was released on bail in order to finish high school, while her brother, Charles, received six years in prison.

When the ruling judge gave a guest lecture at Portland State University, Ford organized thirty protesters to ask questions about putting a teenager in prison for preventing her brother's murder. In response, the judge demanded that the escorting federal marshal arrest Ford, who willingly raised his hands to be cuffed and asked what the charges would be. Instead of arresting him, the judge and the federal marshal left the room.

While the defense coalition grew all over the state of Oregon, demanding that the sister's sentence be vacated, she was raped and impregnated by a guard in the prison. This horrific act was sufficient to release her on bail while her case was on appeal. Her attacker received a paid vacation from the taxpayers. She began studying prelaw but her case repeatedly failed on appeal in the Oregon Supreme Court, and just as she was about to be returned to prison, a federal judge commuted her sentence to time served. The tremendous amount of loud public support bolstered by the Black Panthers most certainly influenced this decision. The family told the press that before the involvement of the Black Panthers, they had no support.

In the end, who wouldn't protect their own brother similarly during an era where the choke hold was a leading cause of death delivered by police officers? The most important questions would be: How much more understanding of her actions would the court have been if she were white? How many things would be different about this case leading up to the confrontation?

Cheryl passed away from organ failure in 2019 after years of trauma. Her sister Martha, now in her sixties, cannot help but cry as she recalls what happened that day. Because the incidents traced back much further.

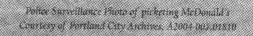

Police Surveillance Photo of picketing McDonald's
Courtesy of Portland City Archives, A2004.005.01810

THE FIGHT FOR ALBINA

*D*espite an ongoing housing crisis, the Portland Development Commission and the City of Portland remained intent on completing its 1956 plan of removing 22 city blocks and demolishing 789 houses in Albina. It built the Memorial Coliseum in 1960, which eliminated the southern edge of Albina. The same year, the largest shopping mall in the United States had also been built, Lloyd Center mall, just past the Coliseum. This created a "white corridor" from downtown to the central eastside. Next, they built I-5, chopping off the west side of Albina in 1964.

The current plan was to add a massive expansion onto the Legacy Emanuel hospital, smack-dab in the center of Albina. More than half of the Albina residents were now targeted for displacement. The displaced people who didn't own property would receive no compensation for their losses and would be pushed further east towards Irving Park, north of Fremont to a new city development project. The Portland NAACP and Urban League responded by organizing residents into pickets and protests for greater tenants' rights. They even brought Dr. Martin Luther King Jr. to speak in Portland about the success of the bus boycotts and Freedom Rides in the South, but it was to no avail.

In 1968, the plan to expand Legacy Emanuel Medical Center and demolish hundreds of Black-owned homes was approved by the city planner board on the grounds that homeowners and residents were compensated for their losses and relocation. After the failed efforts of Emanuel Displaced Persons Association to stop the hospital expansion, the Black Panthers believed that the next best plan would be to ensure full employment of their people. In 1971, the Portland Black Panthers turned their efforts from protecting their homes to securing jobs at the expanding Legacy Emanuel hospital. The police responded by escalating their surveillance on the Panthers.

The city's bureaucratic gears ground along as they planned redevelopment of Albina to better accommodate the white and the wealthy. But the federal government got involved, threatening to pull Portland's funding if the new Model Cities program director couldn't mediate conflicts between the Albina residents, the PDC, and the city.

Simultaneously, against the city's wishes, Viviane Barnett, a subordinate of the Portland Development Commission's Model Cities neighborhood development program, explained to the Black Panthers how they could access public resources. The Panthers used PDC funds to purchase and distribute Christmas baskets throughout the neighborhood. Over fifty years later, Ford recalls how charming and wonderful he found Barnett—it was clear to him that she genuinely wanted to be helpful. But apparently no good deed goes unpunished. For this infraction, Mayor Schrunk allegedly instructed Barnett's boss to fire her. When he refused to fire his subordinate, correctly pointing out that this was an employee doing her job, the mayor fired the head of the Model Cities program.

Model Cities began looking for a new leader. The selection process sought to bring in a new face from out of state who didn't have any baggage in the Albina dispute. Before long, the city hiring committee came across the impressive resume of Charles Jordan. After a series of telephone interviews, they hired Jordan and asked him to relocate to Portland. There was only one problem. The city did not realize before offering him the job that Charles Jordan was Black.

When they found out, the mayor's office was horrified. The mayor's staff couldn't believe that a Black man could impartially mediate conflicts between the city and the Black community—yet this would be his first task. Some residents of Albina were not pleased either. They didn't like the idea of someone being brought in from out of state to do the PDC's bidding.

The militant Black Berets confronted Jordan on the street and kicked in the door to interrupt the city's hiring process meeting. The meeting was supposed to be open to the public, but given the tension, the city had gone to great lengths to keep the public out. Members of the Bureau of Planning were so terrified that some of them *climbed out of the windows*. Some of the Black Berets present that day were still on probation for previous incidents. From then on, Portland Police began detaining R.L. Anderson, the leader of the Black Berets, on any day that planning meetings regarding Albina were scheduled.

Kent Ford and R.L. Anderson were tenuous allies. They had spent several days together in jail and found themselves to be very different people. While they had similar goals, Ford believed that Anderson was going about things all wrong. Each time I point out an injustice against Anderson, Ford is quick to remind me that there is more to the story, such as,

"R.L. was drinking brandy from morning till night. He was full of himself and crooked as shit."

Yet, the lesson of Albina seems clear. When poor people get involved in their neighborhoods, bureaucracy is enacted to remove them from the process. When they continue to show interest in a public process that affects their futures, racist fears are used by law enforcement to ensure that they have no part in the future of their own neighborhoods. When residents become angry at being excluded from this process and react, they are painted as criminals, arrested, and summarily excluded. When residents' desired outcome doesn't happen, the city can point to a public process. But in this case, the PDC enacted an even more insidious plan. They absorbed R.L. Anderson into their bureaucracy to simultaneously sterilize his threat and make him appear like a valued stakeholder.

Indeed, it was Anderson who came to work most closely with the PDC's neighborhood development program. The specter of Portland's racist past seemed to abate—almost. Sitting around the table with the planning board, the stakeholders of Albina and the PDC evaluated the best use for the "blighted area." After a series of proposals—just as the city had feared—director Charles Jordan came to realize that it would be more profitable for the city to maintain and improve existing housing stock in the Albina neighborhood than to destroy it—even if that meant reducing or abandoning the hospital expansion. This plan, of course, was not acceptable. In secret, the city planning board quietly held a poorly attended meeting where it voted to completely remove the hospital's expansion from the federally funded Model Cities program.

If the hospital expansion to repurpose the "blighted" Albina land wasn't part of Model Cities program's jurisdiction, Jordan's conclusions were irrelevant. If Jordan wouldn't act as the PDC's puppet, then the fate of Albina wouldn't be his decision. The PDC had found a loophole that could prevent the Black Panthers from achieving their vision of community control.

Fundamentally, the reasons for this came down to money. The PDC's most profitable development projects were those in Albina—so they ignored Jordan's counsel and research. By this point, the PDC had simply invested too much time, money, and future decisions based on the hospital expansion to abandon or alter it. It's the classic procedure of bureaucratic politics: make a decision without involving the people that it negatively impacts.

In vain, neighborhoods met and voted on their own policy plans for how they would like to be developed. But the city did not adopt a single one of them. This behavior only reinforced the Black Panther's idea of government as an occupying force in their own neighborhoods.

While the city wouldn't budge, the Black Panthers were able to establish a few small concessions with Legacy Emanuel Medical Center. In 1971, the hospital signed an agreement to work closely with displaced residents and the PDC and city planning board to reduce the negative impact of its growth. Despite this, when impacted neighbors did pursue funds for their losses and displacement, the city simply denied them or undercompensated them for their property.

Simultaneously, the city undermined the resistance by further absorbing key members into a bureaucracy that didn't share their interests. R.L. Anderson—a year after angrily disrupting a city board meeting—was voted onto a federally funded advisory board and then elected to become the representative to the city planning department. He mediated discussions between the police and Albina and advised on matters of planning and development. It almost seemed like the tides were turning. But, when Anderson was voted treasurer of the Portland Metropolitan Steering Committee, all hell broke loose as he tried to do his job. Weeks before the deadline, because of prior criminal charges including "assault with a deadly weapon" and "illegal possession of a firearm," no one would underwrite the necessary surety bond for Anderson to receive the $6.2 million in neighborhood development funds. Ford explained to me that he tried to tell Anderson, "You're doing this all wrong. Don't take their money."

Anderson had been elected into office but the establishment bureaucracy could still see him out the door. Denying him the bond was essentially a vote of no confidence because of his criminal past and the color of his skin. Stuck between the difficult decision of forfeiting money for the neighborhood or resigning, tremendous public pressure ensured more stock-in-trade racism. Two weeks into his position, Anderson resigned from the board. The bureaucracy was intent on preventing community control. Despite resigning so his neighbors could receive the neighborhood development funds, a cumulative $14,000 in funding was still withdrawn from the day care program that Anderson ran as well as from the Albina Women's League. Shortly thereafter, Anderson was put in prison on a weapon possession charge by an all-white jury. He had effectively been neutralized. Once again, Ford had a different perspective than my own, explaining that Anderson "insisted on talking to officials on the city payroll—he thought that he could become a suit-and-tie guy. They did this to him but he did this to himself."

Back in reality, the Black Panthers next organized the Black Community Survival Conference (BCSC) in 1972 at Irving Park, with the goal of showing the community opposition and negative impact of the Legacy Emanuel hospital expansion. Never one to miss an allyship, the Panthers created an agreement with the CEO of Legacy Emmanuel where they would receive $1.50 for every sickle cell anemia test they administered, paid for by federal grants. During this time, police surveillance concocted an even stranger conspiracy theory: that the conference was a launching pad to elect radical Black leaders into public office.

While it's common practice today, it was unheard of for public employee unions to be active in the democratic process in 1972. Since police officers are city employees and Portland's police were the first to have a labor union, the PPB slowly normalized the idea for police unions to support and oppose candidates for public office—in addition to intentionally interrupting the democratic process. Portland's Police were the trailblazers of establishing both rights and the idea that police unions would lobby, advocate, and endorse candidates in an election.

Fearing "the worst," one city councilman got so worked up by the BCSC that he walked into a precinct, demanding that the police clear the seven hundred people from the permitted event at the park. The police instead informed him that they had distributed FBI informants throughout the event. Nobody seemed to mention that the conference wasn't breaking any laws or doing anything wrong. Even if the sole purpose of the event was to campaign and elect leaders—which it was not—this would have been perfectly legal behavior that white people conducted every day. Nonetheless, the police had their spies and felt that they could control the Black community. However, from this point forward, for reasons that may be either nefarious or mundane, Portland media completely ceased reporting on the existence of the Portland Black Panthers. Perhaps it was the fact that—besides the scandals emerging in Oakland—the Panther organization was not making national news like they had been for the past five years. Perhaps it was the fact that the lack of reporting in Portland made it much more difficult for the Black Panthers to spread information about their activities. In any event, a media blackout enveloped the remainder of the life of the Party.

Even the Panthers' neutered demands and pleas for Black employment and job training at Legacy Emanuel were ignored. Requests to fairly compensate people who had faced forced relocation were also disregarded. The Black Panthers organized a picket at the hospital in 1973 that included their many white allies. But the administration ignored them. Hundreds of homes were leveled in order to make room for the nineteen-acre expansion, including the bulldozing of the Fred Hampton Memorial People's Health Clinic. The Black Panthers had chosen the clinic location as a political protest, knowing that it was scheduled for demolition. It was a last stand in defending the Black neighborhood. The hospital had agreed to compensate everyone who was displaced but their Black neighbors were skeptical, based on how they had been treated for the past 170 years in Oregon.

After a tense period of extended negotiation, the hospital finally agreed to compensate the Black Panthers with five years of rent at a new office on North Williams Avenue at North Stanton Street. When the Panthers couldn't move out of their current clinic in time, they were granted an extension. The situation seemed amicable until the hospital filed a notice of immediate eviction. The morning after the extension had been granted, Ford arrived at the clinic with a moving truck to find that the county sheriff had shut off their power and broken in, destroying $1,000 worth of vaccines as well as equipment, records, and medications. Ford read them the riot act—a method of shaming people performing antisocial behavior into dispersing—and attempted to flag down a passing TV news van, but it was no use. The Black Panthers had been somehow blacklisted by the media. It was yet another slap in the face.

The new location that the Legacy Emanuel hospital offered for the Fred Hampton Memorial People's Health Clinic had a leaky roof and needed new plumbing and wiring. When the Panthers asked for repairs or funding, the PDC and city planners claimed that they had run out of money and could not make the necessary repairs for the building to be usable. So, instead of the building that the hospital offered—which is now a convenience store covered in graffiti—the Panthers moved the medical clinic into their dental clinic.

Then something even stranger happened. The federal grant that would have paid for the construction of hundreds of new homes in Albina after the expansion, was not funded. The losses were colossal. The City of Portland bulldozed hundreds of homes and the Fred Hampton Memorial People's Health Clinic. So, the city waited for the presidential election and the renewal of funding for the hospital expansion. Instead, Nixon was elected and immediately ended funding for the program. The city and PDC had no way to pay for the hospital expansion it had planned for years. The dust settled and the realizations set in.

When the eldery Leo Warren asked the PDC if the Emanuel Displaced Persons Association could determine the future uses of the bulldozed lots that used to contain their homes, the PDC declined. Why were they bulldozing the clinic and so many houses before they had money to build anything? Fifty years later, the former site of the Panthers' clinic is just a strip of grass on an overflow parking lot, surrounded by more empty lots. The whole demolition of Albina's downtown was for nothing. They created the blight that they were claiming to resolve. Warren commented, "Didn't they have a long-range plan? After all, if your life's investment was smashed to splinters by a bulldozer to make room for a hospital, you could at least feel decent and perhaps tolerable about it; but to have it all done for nothing! Well, what is there to feel? . . . It's funny. I used to think urban renewal was for the people. Now I know it's for places and money and things—not people."

UNDERMINING THE CHAPTER

*T*hrough a combination of fear, intimidation, infiltration, snitch-jacketing, infighting, and outright murder from both the police and each other, the Black Panthers lost 80 percent of their membership by the early '70s. Many chapters completely collapsed under the weight of paranoia by 1972. Aside from that, the Party was changing rapidly. In the span of two years Huey P. Newton went from saying that the Black Panther Party would never run a candidate for office to running his cofounder, Bobby Seale, for the mayor of Oakland and Elaine Brown for city council. Many remaining local Black Panther chapters were closed by the national office, demanding that the memberships move to Oakland to create a greater stronghold in the city and elect candidates, but Portland ignored this and continued doing what they had always done. Not getting involved in the fracas is likely what resulted in their relative longevity.

In order to learn more about communism, members of the Black Panther Party from various chapters, including Portland, traveled to the People's Republic of China in 1972. Traveling to China from the United States was not possible at the time due to poor relations between the countries, so the Panthers planned to travel to Beijing through Vancouver, Canada. However, upon reaching the Canadian border, they were refused entrance by the Canadian government because they feared trouble from the Black Panthers. Undaunted and all too familiar with negative reception, the Panthers rerouted their trip. While most members recount the trip as disappointing—China was far from the communist political utopia that they had come to believe it was—the Panthers did learn quite a bit about Chinese acupuncture. The Panther delegation to China came home and implemented acupuncture in Black Panther clinics, teaching these methods of medicine to poor communities in cities all over the United States. The Panthers even used the five-point ear method as a means of treating drug addiction.

Also in 1972, after all media in Portland completely stopped reporting on Black Panther activity, the FBI's tactics went from inconvenient and disruptive to bone-chilling. The occasional trips to Oakland for funerals, rallies, conferences, or occasions where a Portland Black Panther representative was expected, became more and more frequent—to the point that they would wear down even the most disciplined individuals. Then the FBI seized upon a fantastical narrative that the Panthers were about to go to war, working with local police to spread it.

That year, the Portland Police released a report about the Portland Black Panthers. Sourced from the findings of an anonymous confidential reliable informant (CRI)[68] the police used to infiltrate the Black Panthers, the CRI claimed

---

68 During public hearings on spying in 1996, police admitted to obtaining information by paying CRIs, agents, and volunteer informants. They admitted to spying on residents for offenses such as "suspicion of trespassing." When the Red Squad continued to surveil activists who had committed no crimes, Circuit Court Judge Michael Marcus ordered that they cease tracking law-abiding citizens in 2000. The law was changed the following year under the PATRIOT Act and further expanded under the Obama administration, not only to make spying on any citizen legal, but to create the largest spy network in the history of humanity.

that the Panthers' programs were a smokescreen to harass city bureaus and that they sought to cause chaos instead of building a community movement. The informant also told the police that Kent Ford brought him into his home to show off the Panthers' weapons arsenal, with the implied purpose of starting a war. Ford denies any of this ever happening.

The FBI was convinced that Percy Hampton's trips to Oakland were actually for the purpose of transporting guns and dynamite across state lines—a felony. Once again, they had no evidence to support this claim but they distributed the rumor in his files regardless. When I asked Hampton if there was a kernel of truth to this, like the weapons stockpile that the FBI claimed was hidden both in Ford's apartment and in Panther headquarters, Hampton almost laughed before saying, "None. They didn't find anything at any point." When the *Oregonian* asked Hampton about this, he explained, "I went to California a few times. That was my job. I was in charge of newspaper circulation. Did I transport guns or dynamite across state lines? I was young and stupid, but I wasn't that young and stupid." When I asked him who might have given the FBI this impression, Hampton had some ideas, "I knew who we believed were informants and stayed away from them." In *Racial Matters: The FBI's Secret File on Black America, 1960–1972*, Kenneth O'Reilly claims that there were a total of 67 informants in the Black Panther Party. But William A. Cohendet, the FBI special agent in San Francisco assigned to the Panthers, told Roz Payne in a 1999 interview that *none* of the informants were useful. Indeed, a "Special Duty Report" was filed in Portland on June 23, 1970, where an anonymous police informant claimed to have been tailing Kent Ford, decorated Vietnam war veteran Panther deputy minister of defense Tommy Mills, and Percy Hampton for two weeks. The police had no way to verify the truth of the claims, which were merely that the informant had tried to give a .22 revolver and an old shotgun to Ford, who declined the offer, brought the informant to his home to show him a "large closet in the kitchen" allegedly full of guns, and "[informant] provided no solid information." Ford has always disputed these claims and the police never found any evidence of the violent insurgency that they kept trying to pin on the Panthers.

The trouble with police utilizing CRI's for "intelligence gathering" is that they are almost always working under duress, either seeking a plea bargain or some other form of compensation, and their information is rarely reliable. Worse, the police have almost no way of verifying the information that is fed to them. As a result, a CRI is pressed to produce "something of value" in return for leniency. And, realizing that the police have little means of verifying their information, CRIs often lie or exaggerate.

It is because of bad intelligence and hearsay like this that police shakedown people associated with the Panthers. First, they create these narratives and then investigate them to prove their stories to be accurate. In one case, Oregon State Police arrested Panthers Joyce Radford, Mary Campbell, and Susan Jane Beckard with sixteen others on charges of grand larceny because a gas station clerk claimed that an auto battery, tire chains, and shotgun shells were missing after they filled up their gas tanks. It's a classic racist case of what's missing from the story: the stolen items were not found in their vehicle and there was only hearsay to justify the arrest. Yet, the news story about this arrest running in the *Oregonian* could cement the police's narrative that these were "dangerous" lawbreakers with guns.

Hampton was barely twenty and circumstances like this are enough to keep anyone constantly looking over their shoulder. So, the Panthers attempted to focus on their mission and go about their business as best they could instead of reacting to the people that Ford refers to as "those three-letter guys."

Possibly dating as far back as 1905,[69] the Portland Police developed an anti-communist unit dubbed the "Red Squad." In 1934, Portland Police began hiring agent provocateurs to infiltrate and destabilize left-wing political organizations. The provocateurs suggested acts of violence during planning meetings, and the police would then use this "intelligence" to violently crack down before protests, claiming knowledge of protesters' "violent plans." The city wouldn't acknowledge the existence of the Red Squad for many years and when its existence was proven, the city agreed to disband it several times. Instead, the police merely changed its name to "Criminal Intelligence Division" while it was surveilling the Oregon American Civil Liberties Union and when they were caught again, they changed its name to the "Criminal Intelligence Unit."[70] The Red Squad spied on organizations

---

69 Some accounts claim that the Red Squad was formed in 1905, though if it did exist then, it was unofficial. In its inception, the Red Squad was funded by businesses who wanted to know which of their employees were "communists" and had intentions to unionize.

70 When the police again agreed to disband CID in 1986, the police clarified that it had never targeted groups, individuals, or monitored peaceful events, even though all evidence suggested that this was false. In 1992, CID Officer Sewert was assigned to specifically spy on radicals and subversives, going

including the Panthers while undermining the political activities of its citizens. Similar in fashion to the tactics of the FBI's COINTELPRO, the Red Squad set out to discredit radical politics and protect the status quo. Over the span of at least ninety years it never ceased operations. In a 2011 interview, Michael Munk, author of *The Portland Red Guide* and a professor of history, summarized that the Red Squad never significantly changed its goals or function since its early days, seventy years ago. The Red Squad interrogated members of the Industrial Workers of the World—whose bodies were later found in the river.[71] Similar to the FBI's tactics of "any means necessary," the Red Squad sought to undermine the police's political enemies and CRIs were a vital component of that.

Some of the spying on the Black Panthers was truly bizarre. Once, the Black Panthers met with a white woman in charge of a day care to resolve the hundreds of complaints against her. In a 2022 interview, Ford described this day care as "operating a preschool to prison pipeline." The Panthers showed up for the meeting at the appropriate time, but the director did not. Instead, an individual that Ford now believes to be a potential informant confronted him. They had an unsavory history and a scuffle ensued. When fellow Panther Jeff Fikes got involved in the confrontation, one of the

so far as to submit a report about the groups that were creating the civilian review board of police. Four years later, Douglass Squirrel, an underweight massage therapist who had been profiled and surveilled by police for years, won a $2,000 award for violation of his civil rights. See *Bicycle Culture Rising* for more information on how confidential relative informants and the Red Squad attempt to control culture change in the city of Portland.

71 Michael Munk, *The Portland Red Guide: Sites & Stories of Our Radical Past* (Ooligan Press, 2011).

men who had been posing as a day care employee suddenly identified himself as an undercover police officer. Soon, the police chief appeared. Seemingly, a confrontation was expected. As Ford explains, "We will never know the depths of treachery going on in that place." In any event, the police never managed to prove the absurd claims that they made about the Panthers' extorting the day care nor the Panthers' supposed impending war. We will never know what the police expected to happen that day or what their informants told them because the files were woefully incomplete and much of the information was redacted.

In Oakland, changed by his time in prison, Huey P. Newton had established new habits—chief among them was robbing crack dealers. Newton described these like he was Robin Hood, robbing from the wealthiest members of the poor community to fund Black Panther schools. Slowly losing his grip on reality, he began forcing his inner circle to read

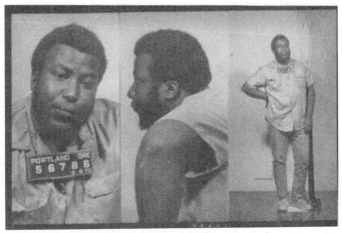

An expressive Jeff Fikes after being arrested

mobster narratives instead of political theory. Around this time, Newton also developed a cocaine addiction. Rumors began to circulate in the press about Newton's lavish top-floor condo and sports cars. Next, allegations surfaced that Newton was stealing funding from Black Panther schools to pay for this lifestyle. Robbing drug dealers seemed less wholesome in this light. This was all too much for Percy Hampton, who had believed idealistically in the mission of the Black Panthers. Hampton felt misled, became disillusioned with the Party, and resigned. When I asked him about events following his resignation, he said that this betrayal caused him to completely cease paying attention to the movement.

Despite these incredible setbacks, in 1973, the Portland Black Panthers helped open an additional clinic inside St. Andrew Catholic Church in Northeast Portland. It was intended to help patients during hours when their own clinic on Williams Avenue was closed. Then something unexpected happened: the FBI began urging Multnomah County to open "competing clinics."

Despite a standing ovation after a funding proposal presentation, the Fred Hampton Memorial People's Health Clinic did not receive any money. Instead, the Albina Health Clinic opened in 1973 and received $170,000 from the same grant. It's a peculiar idea to take the Panthers' approach of community protection and co-opt it in this manner. While it achieves a similar outcome, it dilutes the message. Many of the volunteer doctors and dentists found that the other clinics were not actually serving people in need, but college students and peaceniks. It was as if marginalized people were not comfortable in other free clinics. On top of that, the volunteer doctors and dentists preferred the Fred Hampton Memorial People's Health Clinic because it was achieving what other free clinics only gave lip service to—helping thousands of people in need. Perhaps, as Hampton explained to the *Oregonian*, the difference was that the Panthers provided more than just healthcare: "We were talking about holding the government accountable for poverty, for the lack of affordable healthcare, for the way urban renewal was eating away at the Black parts of town, and especially for the fact that the cops weren't being held accountable for violence." However, the Panthers' message of intersectional politics was catching on elsewhere.

Seemingly in response to the Black Panthers' demand of "control of our neighborhoods," city counselor Neil Goldschmidt was elected mayor in 1973 and did exactly that: he shifted Portland city government power to neighborhood associations. However, these new neighborhood power structures never reached out to the Black Panthers, despite the fact that the Panthers predated them. Nonetheless, in 1974, this restructured city hierarchy and Goldschmidt's activist coalition was able to defeat the state of Oregon's Mount Hood Freeway project and I-505, saving thousands of homes from demolition.

Next, Goldschmidt took the federal funding for the freeway and enacted a gas tax to create transportation options, including free public transportation downtown. He removed a highway along the Willamette River and replaced it with a gigantic park. Goldschmidt invested in the inner city so it became the most desirable place to live while the suburbs were more difficult to access and had fewer amenities. He set out to establish social services and create community accountability for the Portland Police Department and he transferred control of the police to Charles Jordan, the first Black city commissioner in Portland's history. But, as Ford is forever quick to remind me, most of this was just for show. Jordan couldn't stop racial profiling, discrimination, or even effectively get the police to behave—a problem that plagues Portland to this day. Still, Goldschmidt's social programs worked. Crime in Portland under Goldschmidt reduced progressively through the 1970s and the Environmental Protection Agency named Portland the most livable city in America in 1975, despite having one of the highest unemployment rates in the United States.

Yet, the part that makes the least sense is the cost-benefit analysis of Portland city government prior to Goldschmidt. In today's dollars, each home pays average property taxes of over $3,000 so removing three thousand homes costs Portland $10 million in annual income while creating a public works project that costs hundreds of millions in construction and maintenance and never becomes fiscally solvent. Even just pavement maintenance on an ever-expanding metro area often requires financing through bond measures and is not paid for through gas taxes, as was originally intended. The tax "general fund" has to step in to pay for the most politically volatile, yet nonpartisan issue: potholes. Today, if the PDC had not destroyed the homes and businesses in Albina, the city would have an additional $2 million in its budget every year. Charles Jordan was right. Over the next fifty years, the failed "blight" project cost the city around $620 million between lost income and expenses, in addition to an eternal financial black hole.

When it comes down to it, it was neighborhood community activists like the Black Panthers that got Goldschmidt elected. Social service neighborhood organizations like the Panthers *doubled* in the ensuing years. Soon Goldschmidt was in charge of Model Cities, the program that had bulldozed hundreds of Black homes in Albina. Goldschmidt ensured that PDC plans had to be cohesive with neighborhood associations' plans and he filled the new city department with sympathetic allies, those who understood neighborhood activism. If these changes had been implemented when the Panthers demanded them, the residents of Albina would still have their homes.

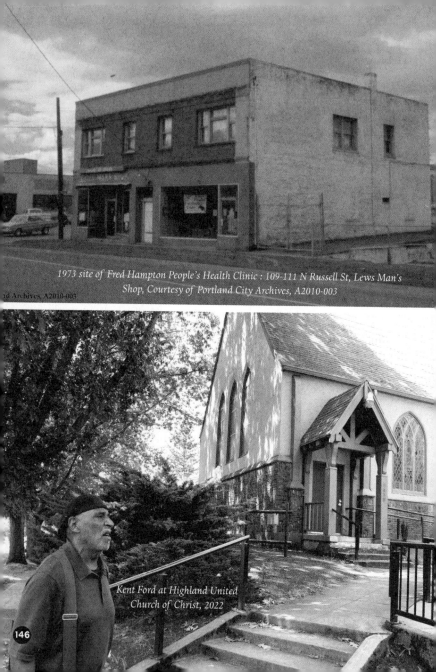

1973 site of Fred Hampton People's Health Clinic : 109-111 N Russell St, Lews Man's Shop, Courtesy of Portland City Archives, A2010-003

Kent Ford at Highland United Church of Christ, 2022

RESISTANT CULTURE

Relentless spying and harassment continued to dwindle the Black Panthers' ranks. By 1975, there were only five members left in Portland, though several former members contributed when and where they could. A new program to send a weekly van to prisons and keep prisoners company had to be abandoned. Sadly, without enough members, the Panthers also had to end the free breakfast program. In a story all too common among the Panthers, the federal government countered the Panthers by offering the same service with greater budgets. It's hard to condemn the federal government for feeding healthy food to hungry children and expanding their own free breakfast program in schools by over 500 percent during this time period, but it acted to undermine the work being done in the community, by the community. The Portland Public School system began serving a remarkably similar breakfast to what the Panthers served. In any event, the Portland Panthers had shown exactly how to feed over one hundred children free breakfast every morning with no funding and had effectively embarrassed the government into adopting similar policies. The missing piece was the intersectionality of the various programs and the underpinning ideology.

Still, smaller ranks couldn't shrink the Panthers' presence. They were invited to share facilities and equipment with Kaiser Permanente in a larger clinic with more operating rooms on North Russell Street at North Flint Avenue. They accepted and moved in, but as the Panthers applied for a Portland Metropolitan Steering Committee (PMSC) grant, another "competing clinic" emerged. The Panthers learned that the very grantor that they were communicating with—who had enthusiastically told them to expect a response soon—was now planning on opening his own free dental clinic to serve the same function as theirs. Worried that a better funded clinic would spell their doom, the Panthers attended the overseeing board meeting to discuss this seeming conflict of interest. The board agreed to investigate the matter and the Panthers picketed the PMSC offices for two weeks. The staff was undeterred so the Panthers moved the picket to the grantor's home on Thanksgiving day. According to Ford, the grantor's wife stepped outside to call them "trash."

Next, when the PMSC hosted a banquet fundraiser, the Panthers purchased a ticket, had it reproduced seven hundred times by a different printer, and distributed those tickets freely. Having twice as many guests as expected, the event was a disaster. But once again, the Panthers were no match for well-connected white government types, and the competing free dental clinic received the grant funding instead of theirs.

In 1978, the U.S. Attorney's Office launched an investigation into a misuse of federal funds allegation at the Fred Hampton People's Free Health Clinic. Sandra Ford cooperated and turned over their records. When reporters started sniffing around and asking questions about any relationship between this investigation and the FBI investigation or the PMSC grantor's competing clinic, the investigation was dropped and explained away as "routine, not politically motivated." The Attorney's Office denied any relationship with the FBI regarding the matter.

But there were bigger problems throughout the city. Even with Charles Jordan as the first Black police commissioner, Black people continued to lose their lives at the hands of law enforcement. Kenneth Allen was killed in a prostitution ring, shot multiple times in the back. The police claimed he had a gun but no such gun was recovered or entered into evidence. A month later, Charles Menefee was killed after a twenty-mile car chase—despite his hands raised in the air to surrender.

In March 1975, police officer Kenneth Sanford shot Ricky Johnson in the back of his head. Johnson and his friends had thrice ordered Chinese food to be delivered by a cab, and the previous two times they had robbed the driver. So, the third time, officer Sanford set up a sting operation, putting on the cabbie's clothes and driving his car. Sanford concealed his firearm in a Chinese takeout box with a hole in the back. When Sanford arrived at the door, one of the boys held it open while Johnson again pointed his handgun at Sanford's head. Except, this time, Sanford identified himself as a police officer and told Johnson to drop the gun. According to witnesses, Johnson did drop the gun and ran. Sanford fired two shots, which he justified on the grounds that he was "afraid for his life." Ricky Johnson had a bullet pass through his skull and get stuck in his cheek. Physical evidence supports the story that Johnson's friends told—the boys ran and Johnson was shot in the back of the head. The only other gun at the scene was inoperable and found more than ten feet away. To this day, the claim that police officers killed someone because they were "afraid for their life" is one of their most effective arguments for defending acts of brutality and murder. None of the officers were called to testify about these or a fourth suspicious death in five months. Neighborhood activists called on the UN to investigate the sheer number of Black people murdered by police in Oregon.

Instead of oversight, the police demanded more money. During a salary negotiation with the city, Portland police union president Stan Peters slammed his gun on the table, shouting, "These are my ground rules." The PPA began running ads attacking council members who attempted to force police accountability. Peters turned the union into a major force in politics—inspiring police forces in other cities to do the same.

Eventually, the multitude of deaths of Black people at the hands of police forced a public inquest. One letter to the *Oregonian* argued that a police inquest into the deaths was unfair because it would make Black residents "privileged." Even Mayor Goldschmidt was afraid of the Portland Police Association and made public statements regarding the inquest that the officers would probably be found innocent anyway. Somehow, during the trial, the conversation became more focused on the fact that the cops used profanity rather than the four murders. Only the sole Black juror voted to convict the officers. Sanford was suspended in 1975 for accepting a gift from a citizen and again in 1977 for the use of illegal drugs. While I wasn't able to find examples of this, Ford insists that Sanford continued to use unnecessary force through his entire career, and that while this was his highest profile incident, it was far from his last.

In 1979, Sandra and Kent Ford's marriage began to deteriorate after they took in a family friend who had two imprisoned parents. The Fords remained committed to supporting the struggle in their community, but more than a decade of this work took a serious toll on them. Kent and Sandra separated but continued to amicably run the Black Panther operation, even after most other chapters in the United States had long ceased to exist.

Soon after, Oregon Health & Science University (OHSU), the landlord of both Black Panther clinics, asked the Panthers to leave. With the wind exhausted from their sails, the Panther clinics did not move or reopen this time. They were again co-opted, this time by the OHSU dental clinic on North Russell Street that continues to this day in the same location. During an interview on KBOO, Percy Hampton explained, "Once we started those programs, the City of Portland decided that they wanted to start the same kind of program. Today, there's fifty thousand children being fed in the City of Portland because the Black Panther Party started the breakfast program that they wanted to counteract . . . which is what we wanted them to do anyway. Same with the health clinics; same with the dental clinics."

Also in 1979, one of the last five Portland Black Panthers, Jeff Fikes, was found shot dead at point-blank range, sitting at the wheel of his wife's car. Weeks prior, Fikes had mocked a cop whose case against the Panthers had been dismissed by a judge because of contradictory statements. The cop shouted at Fikes for all in earshot, "Sooner or later we're going to nail one of you guys." Jeff Fikes's murder was never solved.

Residents protest in front of Emanuel Hospital, 1973
© THE OREGONIAN. All rights reserved. Used with permission.

Kent Ford confronts PDC relocation chief Benjamin Webb on
May 1, 1973 as the Black Panther Clinic is evicted a day before
they agreed upon. © THE OREGONIAN. All rights reserved.
Used with permission.

THE DECLINE

*I*n Oakland, Panther cofounder Huey P. Newton sank further and further from reality. He had become deeply paranoid of FBI infiltration and greatly affected by his time in prison. Now in charge of the Party, Elaine Brown bolstered the Party's support to get Jerry Brown elected and fund a $35 million interstate expansion into Oakland. This was hardly the revolution that people had signed up for and many original members distanced themselves, including Field Marshall Donald Cox. While Portland had successfully removed and fought off interstate expansions in their city to create thriving neighborhoods, in Oakland, the Party bought into partisan politics and freeways as economic drivers. Many members were repelled by this, impatient for the promised revolution. Instead, Newton kicked out numerous high-ranking members for calling for the armed revolution that he had once sought.

The once-charismatic leader was now wholly unpredictable. Saddled with the debilitating cocaine habit—another apparent consequence of COINTELPRO—Newton's mental state continued to devolve. He was brought in on charges of murdering a sex worker. Then he was charged with beating his tailor. Then he ran and hid out in Cuba for three years, only to return and get into a bar fight "with intent to kill." In a move reminiscent of an Italian mob narrative, Newton seemingly sent employees of his Black Panthers' Oakland Community Schools to kill a key witness in his murder trial. The employees were caught and the plot was foiled, but it was one of Newton's darkest days. It was clear that Newton was not himself and the press had a field day, mocking his supposed contradictions. Yet, the Panther cofounder had backers with pockets deep enough to keep him in his penthouse. That's when the allegations surfaced that Newton was funneling Black Panther school funds to his own wallet. Public support for what was left of the Black Panthers essentially collapsed.

Many members rotted in prison. Others, dissatisfied with the unmet revolutionary promises of the Black Panther Party, sought out the more violent Black Liberation Army. Yet, others were locked in years-long legal proceedings to prove their innocence. The effort to reinvent themselves through electoral politics was a failure. Newton's paranoia knew no bounds and he eventually kicked David Hilliard—his best friend since he was eleven years old—out of the Party. Then he kicked out cofounder Bobby Seale, who later said that this move was illegitimate and that he quit because he was burnt out. When membership fell below thirty, Newton returned to his previous life of crime with the remaining Panthers as his criminal syndicate. He robbed crack dealers under the pretense that it was money for the Party. Eldridge Cleaver returned to the United States and became a conservative Republican. In 1988, Bobby Seale published *Barbeque'n with Bobby: Righteous, Down-home Barbeque Recipes*, which many consider the Party's low point because it landed so far from the Black Panther's original intent.

For many, when it was clear that their revolution wasn't happening, they either chose to join the establishment or become yet more radical. The national branch of the Black Panther Party functionally ceased to exist and stopped publishing the newspaper in 1980. Shortly thereafter, as crack cocaine was introduced to poor, Black communities all over the United States, the Portland Black Panther clinics finally shutterd their doors for good. Ford cited burnout and the election of Ronald Reagan as principal causes for their demise, but it seems that COINTELPRO's infiltration of the Portland Black Panthers was just as—if not more—disastrous.

Panther Geronimo Pratt claims that it was the FBI's goal to get Huey P. Newton hooked on cocaine, and if that's true, they were successful. By 1989, Newton was so hooked on cocaine that the drug ran his life until he was murdered in a robbery gone bad.

All Power to the People

The Black Panther Party was quite active in Portland, having both dental and health clinics, providing community education and activism. At the height of their free breakfast program, over 10,000 children were served. Many current programs are based on those they started.

AFTERMATH

*T*he Panther chapter in Portland was over, but Ford was far from finished. There was still more work to do.

One night in March of 1981, some police officers spent their evening running over some possums, collecting the corpses, and calling in for backup to watch and laugh as they deposited possum corpses in the doorway of the Burger Barn, a local Black-owned and frequented establishment. At least some of the officers seemed to believe that this was wrong—or might have negative consequences—because they chose to wait in their cars. Unfortunately, someone that the cops did not know was present was the owners' son, who watched five police cars pull up and saw the entire incident unfold in horror. The officers' message was clear: possum equated to a racial slur and the pile of seven dead possums in the doorway stacked up to a death threat.[72] The owners had seven children—the same number of possum corpses they claim were deposited in front of their restaurant. The officers were overt and publicly admitted to the act afterwards.[73] A clause in the police's union contract protected individual officers from being named in the press or punished publicly.

The cops were bearing more resemblance to a hate group than a police department and Burger Barn owners, George

72 Dating back 150 years, possums were used as death threats against free Black people by white hate groups in the U.S. South. The Powes, who grew up in Missouri and Mississippi, interpreted the possums in this context.

73 Patail, Marty. "The Possums, the Police, and the Burger Barn." *Portland Monthly*, Portland Monthly, 6 Oct. 2020, pdxmonthly.com/news-and-city-life/2020/09/the-possums-the-police-and-the-burger-barn.

and Geraldine Powe, demanded that the police investigate. Before long—utilizing the Internal Affairs Division that the Black Panthers had forced them to create—the department identified which officers were involved, two of which admitted to their involvement.

With seeming impunity, the officers claimed that the Burger Barn was a major hub of criminal activity in Portland, and that this justified their behavior. When that didn't relieve the pressure, the officers explained that depositing the dead possums was an act of frustration and a "prank gone wrong," not a threat. Besides, they said, it wasn't technically a crime.

Horrified, longtime friend of the owners of Burger Barn, Kent Ford, began contacting everyone that he knew in the media. He was frustrated by the slow response and claimed that even the *Skanner*, one of Portland's Black newspapers, had failed to report on the story. But when I checked with the *Skanner*, they were able to pull the reporting from their archives and the person who had taken the photos over forty years ago was still selling ads there today. According to Ford, the story wasn't reported locally until it had gone national. And boy did this story go national.

After intense public outrage, public sympathy rested with the Powes, who believed that this was part of an escalating campaign of harassment from the police designed to scare away their customers and ruin their business. The Powe family had long been financially supportive of their community and people in their neighborhood. They fed and financially supported families in need. According to Ford, "If you had a chicken basket at the Burger Barn, you're in heaven." Seeking to stop this escalation, the owners of the Burger Barn filed a $3.8 million lawsuit against the police.

The two officers, Craig Ward and Jim Galloway, came forward and spoke at a press conference to Black leaders. Nationally, the Klu Klux Klan began using the Burger Barn story as a recruiting tool because the officers were not charged with any crime for their actions. Since the officers had still received no punishment even after they were identified, the KKK suggested that they were bravely standing up as role models.

Outraged, two hundred people with the Black United Front protested at city hall until police commissioner Charles Jordan fired the two officers. Bolstered, the public demanded increased oversight of officers and a citizen review committee. It could have been a huge turning point in Portland's history. Instead, Stan Peters, still president of the PPA, again pointed out that dumping dead possums in the doorway of a Black establishment was (somehow) not a crime. Peters told the *Oregonian* that Jordan "knuckled into the pressure of the opportunists." Jordan began receiving death threats and was assigned bodyguards.

It's clear that Peters was seizing the news cycle for his political goals. Peters sought to reinstate the officers' jobs, forcing their cases to binding arbitration. Next, Peters organized a ballot drive for the police officers' rank and file to fire the police commissioner and raise a vote of no confidence against the chief. He organized a "Cops Have Rights Too" march for public visibility in support of the fired officers, similar to the one organized by the Black United Front a month prior. Dwarfing the march for police oversight, 850 people showed up to support the two fired officers and demand Charles Jordan be fired. Their ranks consisted mostly of off-duty cops, their families, and supporters. Counterprotesters attended with pig heads on spikes. Nonetheless, the political power of the police was clear and the rally was successful.

The police's union arbitrator felt that termination was too harsh and both officers were reinstated to the force. The Ward and Galloway case became the most influential and leading police discipline case in the United States. Not only is it the arbitration decision referred to most often from coast to coast, it's so frequently cited in cases when an officer is terminated for behavior that the precedent is simply referred to as "City of Portland." And now, across the country, when officers are fired for conduct, the courts refer to the cases of Ward and Galloway, and the officers are almost always reinstated. In Portland, the police were successful at creating union contracts where officers had more and more rights with each successive contract renewal. Today, when a police officer shoots someone, they have two days to collude with their union representation, lawyers, and fellow officers to create a version of the story that leaves them with no wrongdoing before they can be interviewed about the incident by the district attorney or their superiors.

The Powe family settled their lawsuit against the police for $69,000 but the stress of these events was too much for Geraldine Powe's heart. She became depressed, withdrawn, and soon passed away from heart failure.

In 1985, responding to a fight between three people in a 7-Eleven parking lot, the police killed Lloyd Stevenson, a Black security guard at Fred Meyer, with a choke hold. The choke hold was banned in response. During Stevenson's funeral, police officers sold T-shirts in the Justice Center break room that said, "Don't choke 'em, smoke 'em." When these officers were fired, the case went to arbitration, the lawyers claimed that the insensitivity was unintentional, and the officers were reinstated.

That same year, the Philadelphia police bombed a row house, killing eleven Black people, including five children.[74] The row house was the home of MOVE, a Black anti-government group in a middle-class residential neighborhood who ate raw food, protested the zoo, planted community gardens, and had once ended up in a shoot-out with the police. After numerous incidents where members were arrested, MOVE was categorized as a terrorist organization.[75] At the time, Philadelphia had one of the largest police forces in the United States and the city ran it without political interference. Mayor Frank Rizzo, a mouthy former officer dubbed the "super cop," was identified as a possible successor for J. Edgar Hoover. MOVE was equally mouthy and unafraid to go to court to defend their rights, despite over 150 arrests. Neighbors began calling the police to the MOVE row house with complaints of roaming animals, lingering odors, strange noises, and naked members wandering the block. The dispute became one about maintaining property values. This culminated in a violent conflict in May of 1985 when the block was evacuated and the city was intent on eradicating MOVE members from their home.

74 Demby, Gene. "Why Have so Many People Never Heard of the Move Bombing?" *NPR*, NPR, 19 May 2015, npr.org/sections/codeswitch/2015/05/18/407665820/why-did-we-forget-the-move-bombing.
75 Read more in *What Was the MOVE Bombing?*, Joe Biel, 2023

During a protracted standoff, the successive mayor gave the go-ahead to drop C-4 plus three cans of fuel on the row house from a helicopter. The alleged goal was to scare MOVE members from their home, but each time the MOVE members attempted to evacuate, barrages of police gunfire drove them to retreat back into their home. Instead, the bomb quickly burned down dozens of neighboring buildings. After twelve hours of flaming horror, Police Commissioner Gregore Sambor declared to Fire Commissioner William C. Richmond, "I would like to let the fire burn, let the bunker burn."[76] There is one surviving adult, several children, and several members who were incarcerated at the time of the bombing. The justification is inconceivable, and the legal battles from the bombing continue nearly thirty years later. Due to these events, Rizzo did not ultimately replace Hoover, but in many ways the MOVE bombing was a brazen escalation from the covert murders of those like Fred Hampton and the clandestine government repression of these movements. Aside from being important as largely forgotten history, the MOVE bombing is perhaps the climax of the U.S. government's conflict with its own citizens.

All was not lost however, and these events kickstarted the next generation of activists. The Powe's granddaughter, who was eleven years old during this polarizing incident, learned some stark lessons in community organizing. Teressa Raiford watched her grandparents feed and nurture the community at the Burger Barn—then the total collapse of

---

76 Drogin, Bob. "Philadelphia Seeks Causes of MOVE Disaster: A Second Look at an Urban Nightmare." *Los Angeles Times*, Los Angeles Times, 20 Oct. 1985, latimes.com/archives/la-xpm-1985-10-20-mn-13910-story. html#:~:text=Then%20a%20white%20dog%20came,%2C%20let%20the%20bunker%20burn."

that social infrastructure. When Raiford's nephew, Andre Dupree Payton, was killed in a gang-related incident in 2010, her life was changed forever. She permanently relocated back to Portland from Texas because there were unanswered questions in her nephew's shooting.

Teressa Raiford founded the nonprofit Don't Shoot PDX and works closely with community leaders to reduce gun violence. In the past ten years, she's run for city council, county commissioner, county sheriff, and ran a write-in campaign during the mayoral runoff election in 2020. Raiford's mayoral bid was strange. She was not on the ballot and insisted that she did not have time to actively campaign but made vague gestures that her write-in campaign was a response to public disapproval for the candidates. According to claims from multiple sources that I could not verify, this was because her campaign manager disliked the inexperienced white candidate set to likely unseat the incumbent mayor. Raiford's write-in campaign inevitably split the vote against her white rival and resulted in the incumbent mayor narrowly remaining in office. In 2022, the sole bipartisan issue in Portland is a strong hatred for the mayor—conservatives think he's in league with the protesters and the left has watched his police attack protesters while struggling with both leadership and communicating clear directives throughout his tenure. When George Floyd was murdered by police in 2020, protests raged in Portland for two hundred days—stopping only when smoke from wildfires made it unsafe to breathe outside. Kent Ford proudly attended every night and criticized others for being more interested in talking to the media than protesting in the streets. The protests also resulted in intense response from police, FBI, and kidnappings of protesters by feds in unmarked vans.[77] The mayor variously complained that he had to do his job and his position on the matter seemed to change depending on the day and whom you talked to. The police's response—including over six thousand incidents of admitted force—was even criticized by the Department of Justice. Raiford worked on a lawsuit that resulted in police tear gas bans on protesters, similar in spirit to the efforts of the Panthers before her.

Today, nationally, officers who are fired for killing innocent people are reinstated to their jobs 25–70 percent of the time, after filing wrongful termination suits. The result is that it's virtually impossible to fire a police officer so most cities don't even try to, even for cause. Further, officers are increasingly disconnected from the communities that they work in. As of 2022, 82 percent of Portland Police live outside of the city, with the majority living in Washington state.

While the former home of the Burger Barn was torn down in 2017, its legacy remains. Realizing that this hate crime somehow resulted in federal inability to fire police officers for cause was the most horrifying revelation of this research. Officer Ward, now retired, told the *Willamette Week*, "It was the biggest mistake of my life. I put the city through hell and brought discredit to the bureau. But it wasn't done out of meanness or racial motivation. It's my fault, and I try to make amends for it every day." He either left out or didn't realize that his actions also resulted in making police officers

77 Dickinson, Tim. "'Illegal Abduction': Portland Protester Sues Feds for Snatching Her off the Street." *Rolling Stone*, Rolling Stone, 23 May 2022, rollingstone.com/politics/politics-news/evelyn-bassi-illegal-abudction-portland-protests-1357279/.

virtually termination-proof. It made me wonder if the Black Panthers could have bolstered public support for Charles Jordan and enacted some actual police oversight instead. But when researching history, you can't get lost in what-ifs. You can only focus on the next chapter.

Kent Ford enthusiastically presenting on a 2022 walking tour of former Panther sites

LEGACY

*I*n 1984, Portland developed a serious gang problem. California gang leaders relocated up north and began recruiting. Over the next forty years, city development continued to push Black people out of Albina. The total number of houses in Albina dropped by 60 percent. The neighborhood went from 49 percent to 33 percent Black as families were forced to move to other neighborhoods. This made gang violence much worse by 2014, as rival gangs were no longer separated geographically, but often lived on the same block or even in the same building. The gang shootings expanded to the suburbs. After a relentless series of shootings in 2014, Jason Washington and DeMarcus Preston created *Take Back the Streets*, a community social bicycle ride attended by 350 people to bring gang leaders together around common problems and reduce violence while getting healthy.[78] Preston's goal is to create "one big gang, one big unit" and he had plans to open a detox home for people who wanted to leave the gang lifestyle. Yet, as real estate prices continued (and continue) to skyrocket since 2006, Portland has had the highest cost of living proportionate to its income in the United States, and Preston hasn't yet been able to meet his goal. Real estate prices also pushed many Black families out of the metro area altogether.

The remedies for this are virtually nonexistent. Since 1979, there have been no more large federal grant programs for neighborhood improvement like Model Cities. This means

---

78 *Groundswell #2: Take Back the Streets.* Microcosm Publishing, 14 Aug. 2021, https://vimeo.com/120739946.

that there is no way to rebuild the Albina neighborhood to its former glory, nor to restore valuable real estate for habitation. The empty lots intended for the expansion of Legacy Emanuel are still just empty lots. To quiet national critics when the PDC sold land to a California developer to build a Trader Joe's in Albina in 2014, the City of Portland created a $138 million fund for Black families to stay in Albina.[79] But eight years later, a third of the budget hasn't been spent and even Mayor Wheeler called it an "abject failure." The simple math is that 1,000 homes were removed and only 76 Black families became Albina homeowners through the program. And there's nowhere for the other 924 families to go. Applications for affordable housing outstrip supply, ten to one. A new construction plan was announced in the South Waterfront with 2,800 units, 59 of which were declared "affordable." Aside from the fact that the legal definition of "affordable" is far beyond what anyone would agree with, the real headline should be "New Housing Complex Offers 2,741 Additional Unaffordable Units."

The property that once was home to the Fred Hampton Memorial People's Health Clinic is now overfill parking for Legacy Emanuel hospital staff. When you look at the property and imagine its former glory, it's hard to imagine how anyone would look at this and think it's being used effectively. As of 2022, there is a plan to build luxury apartments on the site, but when I asked about this on a recent walking tour, several people responded "I'll believe it when I see it."

79 Jaquiss, Nigel. "The City of Portland Tried to Undo Gentrification. Black Portlanders Are Conflicted about the Results." *Willamette Week*, wweek. com/news/2022/05/25/the-city-of-portland-tried-to-undo-gentrification-black-portlanders-are-conflicted-about-the-results/?adsafe_ip=.

Indeed, the more time that I think about all that happened over the past sixty years, it seems that the public misinformation campaign about the Black Panthers launched by the police and FBI is the only thing that could have convinced anyone that valuable yet unused land is better than offering free social services.

While the Portland Black Panthers couldn't singlehandedly solve all of the city's problems in ten years, there are many aspects of their legacy that exist to this day. The Fred Hampton Memorial People's Health Clinic was the longest running Black Panther hospital in the United States. It ran without interruption for over ten years. It serviced thousands of people who had reasons to be hesitant about going to the doctor at all. After all, the hospital was where Black people went to die, not to get help. The Fred Hampton Memorial People's Health Clinic changed that narrative by showing that some doctors did care. It also exposed a population that wasn't receiving care and successfully changed that. Just as it took years of establishing trust to write this book with the Panthers, many patients have a very difficult time trusting white doctors with their healthcare needs. This can be difficult to understand if you are coming from a position of systems working as they are supposed to. But for marginalized people, a trip to the doctor is often much more complicated. A typical visit usually begins with convincing someone that you don't have an STI and that the problems you are describing aren't just for attention—you would like them treated and to receive guidance on how to manage your health.[80] Usually, for marginalized people, it's a struggle to

---

80 Alondra Nelson, *Body and Soul: The Black Panther Party and the Fight against Medical Discrimination* (University of Minnesota Press, 2013).

convince your doctor to order the tests that you need and to take your problems seriously. The Fred Hampton People's Free Clinic changed that for Portland. Over the past eighteen years, I routinely heard accounts of Black people whose first—and sometimes only—positive healthcare experience was at the Black Panthers' clinic in Portland.

The greatest legacy of the Portland Black Panthers, however, is the creation of the Oregon Health Plan (OHP), a form of single-payer healthcare in Oregon for people who earn too much to be on medicare but too little to purchase insurance. Floyd Cruse, who loved to give speeches about his time in the Black Panther Party, mentioned this casually to me in 2006, like it was a fact that everyone knows. However, he passed away in 2015 and tracing the relationship was much more complicated because I couldn't find any documentation about it in any of the existing records. Untangling this relationship required years of digging and asking dozens of historians and elderly people to comb their memories for the various details as they could recall them. The breakthrough came by offering Jon Moscow a list of people associated with the program and him discussing each of them with Sandra Ford.

In 1969, the first Portland Black Panther clinic was opened in partnership with Health/RAP, who specialized in demonstrating how Portland healthcare is complicit in oppressing the poor. Health/RAP's Jon Moscow, a white ally of the Panthers, recognized the immense neglect that Black people received in healthcare—as well as the opportunity to embarrass the city for this. Moscow seized the opportunity to build healthcare reform into the public dialogue and state agenda. This is why Moscow gave Ford that list of every doctor that he knew would be willing to volunteer for the Panthers' clinic. And the rest is history.

Jon Moscow—working with public health advocates Robert Spindel and Don Hamerquist—found a unique way to influence the healthcare conversation and assisted racial justice in healthcare. TheFred Hampton Memorial People's Health Clinic became so effective that other clinics were referring patients to the Black Panthers for superior care. When the FBI urged Multnomah County to open competing free clinics to undermine the Panthers, ironically giving the Black Panthers what they wanted all along. The battle to make the Panthers obsolete and unnecessary slowly led to the government providing adequate services, including healthcare.

In fact, important breakthroughs were happening as a result of the Black Panther Clinics. Dr. Ralph Crawshaw hung around the clinics to observe and collect data. Dr. Crawshaw observed what Jon Moscow set out to expose—that there were poor populations not being accounted for in state data. Sandra Ford remembers Dr. Crawshaw being interested in the Black Panther clinics to demonstrate demand for healthcare from people who weren't visible in the system. Dr. Crawshaw had a vision for a state health program for people with income limits, studying healthcare in prison as well.

After Dr. Crawshaw had spent ten years collecting data with his own organization, Oregon Health Decisions, he met ER doctor John Kitzhaber. In 1978, Kitzhaber moved from medicine to politics, and Dr. Crawshaw stayed in Kitzhaber's ear, talking about the many populations that were not being served by Oregon's healthcare system. The Fred Hampton

Memorial People's Health Clinic was evicted by OHSU in 1980, but the data that Dr. Crawshaw had collected there to prove his thesis would serve a vital purpose. Righting some of the injustices done to those like Henrietta Lacks, this time the information collected was used to help Black people and the poor, not just the medical establishment.

Seven years after the closing of the Fred Hampton Memorial People's Health Clinic, a seven-year-old died because the state's medicare board no longer funded bone marrow transplants. Advocates like Dr. Ralph Crawshaw made sure that this preventable tragedy was in the news. Aghast, the public erupted into a debate over what healthcare should pay for.

In response, from his new position as governor, Neil Goldschmidt created a healthcare workgroup to decide who should be covered, what is paid for, and how it would be paid for—and once again his advisors were community organizers and activists with backgrounds in the Panthers or similar groups. The workgroup spent four years investigating, then wrote a report that stressed similar conclusions to that of the Black Panthers. They concluded that it is a better investment for the state to pay for healthcare than to let people languish without care and make trips to the emergency room after it's too late, or in government-speak, "it [is] rational for the state to identify the most important health services and to make those services available to a larger number of underserved residents." Over the next six years, Dr. Ralph Crawshaw convinced doctor turned governor John Kitzhaber that the solution was OHP—for the state to insure 120,000 people to access basic care. In a 2022 interview, Kitzhaber explained, "We wanted to make sure that there's equity in how these dollars are allocated. There were three hundred thousand uninsured kids who were 'invisible.' We tend to fund what is immediate and visible. That didn't seem fair to me and that was the basis of making everyone visible. We shared this belief that the invisible people needed to be given a voice—so [Crawshaw] said, 'Why don't you go out and talk to the invisible people?' It was an equity and resource allocation plan." On its face, thirty years later, this statement doesn't sound that radical but the concepts were unheard of at the time. It reads almost like a response to the Black Panthers' 1972 update to their Ten-Point Program, "We Want Completely Free Health Care For All Black and Oppressed People."

Dr. Ralph Crawshaw realized that they would need to build public support for such a radical vision. Kitzhaber was moving from the state legislature to the governor's seat and this allyship would prove powerful. In our 2022 interview, Governor Kitzhaber recalled, "Ralph had a very wry sense of humor. When the battle lines were clear between people who wanted us to insure everything and those who thought we had limited resources, Ralph said something like, 'I watch all the acrimony in Salem and I shake my head because all of us want the same things.' Then he went out and he demonstrated that in town hall meetings around Oregon. This was particularly instructive to me throughout my political career. You can achieve things that seem impossible."

Indeed, Dr. Crawshaw organized ten different town hall meetings all over the state of Oregon and he found that the concerns and problems were the same in all regions of the state, starting with prevention—just like the Black

Panthers had identified in their clinics. Governor Kitzhaber explained, "I saw people everyday in the ER that suffered from accumulated results of social failures—mold in their homes that gave them asthma, poor diets from a food desert, domestic violence because of poverty, and I'd treat their medical problems—before sending them back to the same conditions. I started seeing people in the ER that I knew— people who had suffered violence or abuse or dissolution of families, people who, through no fault of their own, could no longer put food on the table. You are just as responsible for his stroke as his blood pressure. What Ralph convinced me of is this academic model is actually a very human issue. You need to talk to people, get out of your head, and out of the Capitol. The bill passed [easily] because we could tell [representatives] that we had gone to their district and asked their constituents what they needed."

Oregon Health Plan was an immediate success. Unpaid debts to hospitals dropped 16 percent. By 2000, the number of people covered had doubled. Today, now supported by Obamacare, the program covers over one million people, 26 percent of Oregon's population, including 60 percent of Oregon's children.

OHP is far from the Portland Black Panthers' only lasting accomplishment. Historians focus mostly on the failures of the Panthers, their iconic fashion posturing with rifles, and the years of gradual demise. This causes them to miss the fact that Panthers were shockingly successful at establishing most of their Ten-Point Program and survival programs during their tenure, with many of these programs and campaigns lasting successfully into the present.

The local, state, and federal government adopted nearly all of the Black Panther Party programs—without giving them credit, of course. After embarrassing the federal government about how it did not treat sickle cell anemia the same way that it did genetic diseases that primarily affect white people, federal funding and studies were created as a result of the Black Panthers' efforts to cure and prevent sickle cell.[81] Because of the Panthers' work, the first cases of sickle cell are being cured at the National Institutes of Health by transplanting stem cells from relatives. Virtually all of the Black Panthers' survival programs were adopted as well: free breakfast programs for children, neighborhood community control, citizen bureaus to oversee police, free clinics, free dentists, employment programs for Black people, housing programs,[82] and equal employment education programs. Even after the Black Panther clinics were closed, numerous former volunteers had been trained to perform pelvic examinations and gonorrhea screenings. Some of the volunteers, including Sandra Ford, would go on to have careers in healthcare as lab technicians and dental assistants.

While some of the Black Panthers' demands were less tangible, the only ones categorically ignored were the exemption of Black men from military service and the releasing

81 In 2019, the Centers for Disease Control and Prevention added an additional $1.2 million in funding to collect data and continue to help people with sickle cell. Alondra Nelson, *Body and Soul: The Black Panther Party and the Fight against Medical Discrimination* (University of Minnesota Press, 2013).

82 Jaquiss, Nigel. "The City of Portland Tried to Undo Gentrification. Black Portlanders Are Conflicted about the Results." *Willamette Week*, wweek. com/news/2022/05/25/the-city-of-portland-tried-to-undo-gentrification-black-portlanders-are-conflicted-about-the-results/?adsafe_ip=.

of all Black men from jails and prisons. The Portland Black Panthers fought for years to establish and protect "Decent Housing Fit For The Shelter Of Human Beings," with varying levels of success. Of course, "We Want An Immediate End to Police Brutaility and Murder of Black People" could certainly use some work, but it has seen renewed vigor and public pressure in recent years. For the first time in U.S. history, we are seeing convictions for police officers who kill Black people. Indeed, the Portland Black Panther Party was so successful because it could effectively build innumerable coalitions with white allies who saw the value in its work. In addition to how the federal government came to see the Black Panthers' ideas as good ones to implement—after going to incredible lengths to destroy the organization—the most valuable lesson of the Panthers is that intersectional movements are stronger than groups working in isolation. By building powerful coalitions, you can accomplish your goals.

The history of Portland's Black Panthers should be taught in the textbooks of public high schools, yet the largest file kept about them by the city government are the surveillance files in the public archives. When the City of Portland began installing sidewalk plaques to commemorate the history of Albina, the Black Panther markers were not at the former sites of the demolished Black Panther clinics. It's heartbreaking to think about for too long. The city had twisted this mutual aid organization until it was wracked with paranoia and infighting.

In 2022, I asked Percy Hampton if he ever sought out his FBI files. Hampton had, and he had a pragmatic reason for doing so. "I wanted to see what they got on me," he said.

Hampton had some bumps in the road. After leaving the Black Panthers, he got into a fight with an ex and later spent six months in prison for a burglary conviction in 1979. The way that police manufactured the hostile confrontation with him when he was just a bespectacled teenager had tempered him, and it took ten years to get agency back in his own life. The fact that the FBI had—seemingly falsely—accused him of smuggling guns and dynamite across state lines in his file didn't help.

As Hampton was trying to get his life back in order in 1980, he went to work in construction. There was a promising job at a nuclear power plant, but the job required a federal security clearance. Hampton needed to know what his future employers would find when they did a background check on him. So he requested his own files. All told, what he found wasn't so bad, but he knew the FBI's propensity for hyperbole. He told KBOO, "FBI agents would come to our house and ask me if I'd been anyplace lately and showed me a picture of me and say, 'This is some guy doing guard duty at chapter headquarters in Oakland. I heard it was you.'"[83] Hampton told me, "They exaggerate everything but security up there looked through it and nothing made it seem like I was going to blow up the damned nuclear plant."

Hampton received federal clearance and was hired. He went on to become the union president of 1,100 people. He didn't talk about being a Black Panther much—he figured it would concern his boss. It was in his distant past. "A couple of kids came to my union for a job and they reminded me that I fed them through the breakfast program." So, Hampton

83 "Portland Black Panther Party." *KBOO*, 9 July 2016, https://kboo.fm/media/5033-portland-black-panther-party.

looked out for and reached out to kids that the Portland Black Panthers served in the breakfast program and offered to help them out with work in his union. He worked there for fourteen years, until the plant was closed and he eventually retired. Now that he's retired, he's more comfortable talking about his former involvement with the Black Panthers and comforted by the knowledge that the wild-ranging accusations in his FBI file didn't affect his later life.

Kent Ford, on the other hand, was curiously not interested in his own FBI files. This seemed strange to me, so I probed him about it extensively, failing to produce a satisfactory answer. But over the years, as I worked more intensively on this project, the United States saw the emergence of mainstream "false information with the intention to deceive public opinion." The FBI's disinformation playbook is adapted from the Russian disinformation office's strategies, developed in 1923, and is now used by everyone from the Pizzagate[84] conspirators to flat-earthers. Russian President Vladimir Putin, who learned disinformation from his time in the KGB, has also increasingly brought these strategies to the United States over the past twenty years. Putin utilized the psychology that "Disinformation breeds paranoia, which breeds apathy, which forms absurdist theories and lands the public in a cloud of cynicism. Cynics eventually become futilists. Futilists are apathetic; they are not interested in forcing social change. It's a very effective form of social control." I even fell for the Soviet

---

[84] The claim in 2016 that leaked emails from a high-ranking political official demonstrated "proof" that "cheese pizza" was coded language for "child pornography" and "proved" that a basement was full of child sex slaves in a pizza restaurant in DC. This culminated in a man driving from North Carolina to Washington, DC with an assault rifle to rescue the alleged sex slaves.

claim that the CIA had created the AIDS virus to control the U.S. population.[85] It was juicy and there were enough accurate and related stories that it pointed to. The problem is that, like any fake news, it's false—and thus it's not only a distraction; it's divisive and concerning; it's designed to make people like Ford feel stagnant and defeated.

I came to understand that by relying upon his own facilities, Ford prevents these worrying ideas from directing him. Ford and I both know that his FBI file will contain endless disinformation from confidential reliable informants, offering bad intelligence for deals. It will point fingers at his friends, regardless of the truth. It's a distraction. It offers no substantial answers. In this light, I slowly understood why Ford didn't want to wade through hundreds of pages of disinformation in order to evaluate his life. At Black Panther conferences, the most common topic is guessing which members were COINTELPRO infiltrators, which is a very effective form of neutralizing the would-be activists. Ford, on the other hand, remains focused on the future, instead of on the past.

Similarly, the public doesn't understand the Black Panther Party because of disinformation that was fed to them. Oscar Johnson told KBOO, "I had a young man call me a nazi. I had to explain the Ten-Point Program to him. He was—through ignorance—didn't really know what we did. And now young people seem to want to know and the changes we made and the changes we went through."

Unfortunately, sometimes the FBI brings the fight to the Fords. Kent and Sandra's son, Patrice Lumumba Ford,[86]

85 *Operation InfeKtion: How Russia Perfected the Art of War* | NYT Opinion, 2018 youtube.com/watch?v=tR_6dibpDfo
86 Named after the democratically elected leader of the Congo who was

was arrested on terrorism charges for attempting to travel to Afghanistan in 2001. He and six others were traveling to help with a relief effort and were instead swept up in by the Joint Terrorism Task Force. The seven men were accused of intending to fight alongside the Taliban against the United States. Lumumba was the last of the seven to sign a plea bargain, and thus received an eighteen-year sentence. As a result, Ford began pounding the pavement, spending the next eighteen years campaigning for his son's release. For years, "Free Lumumba" posters graced every other telephone pole in Portland. These posters were my first introduction to the Portland Black Panthers. Lumumba was finally released in 2018, after more than seventeen years in prison.

•   •   •

I figured that I knew the answer, but I asked Ford why he didn't end up like Tom Hayden, the '60s radical who left the revolution to take over a seat on the Senate. He explained, "Electoral politics—people like Obama that go into it, they do good at it but, in a sense, their hands are tied. The infrastructure is designed to water you down. I wish them all the luck in the world. My hat's off to them. I'd help them, knock on doors, but what happens is that they get into the Capitol with the right-wing Republicans and vote against the welfare bill, even though you were on welfare yourself. When Jesse Jackson was elected and ripped off Fred Hampton's rainbow coalition idea, I stopped being so fixated on color and

murdered by a death squad on order from President Eisenhower. "The C.I.A. and Lumumba." *The New York Times*, The New York Times, 2 Aug. 1981, nytimes.com/1981/08/02/magazine/the-cia-and-lumumba.html focused more on their politics and their treachery. I always figured that I'll stay here in the community with the people." In terms of having your hands tied, I immediately thought of the two congressmen that received documents about the true nature of the FBI's activity in 1971, and—instead of revealing these crimes to the public—chose to quietly return them to the FBI.

However, when I ask Kent Ford about his legacy, he's quick to direct me to other activists, people that he claims have accomplished more or are more important than him, by his evaluation. When I asked Percy Hampton about how he feels about the Portland Black Panthers' accomplishments, he thought about it for a minute, before responding. "I like that I am a part of history. Every time I turn around, I see more kids that we fed . . . I feel proud of that."

Neither Ford nor Hampton were aware of the role that they played in the creation of OHP. Even as I inform Ford of this, he tells me about another activist that he respects, doing good work in his community. When I ask him about his class-action lawsuit that resulted in community control of police, he redirects to how much more it should have accomplished. Ultimately, as he puts it, Probasco's reforms are "just another neoliberal show." Batons were merely replaced by tasers. The Internal Affairs Division ignores complaints to this day.

However, by starting far to the left, the compromised results were successful reforms. When liberal advocates begin by asking for reform, the result is almost always compromising with nothing. So, while Ford has a point, every day that you don't get clubbed in the skull by the baton of a cop high on stolen cocaine, thank a Portland Black Panther.

When I asked Hampton how he feels about the sheer number of Black Panther programs that the government has adopted, he explains, "We took a 'wait and see' approach to find out how it will go." When I point out that it's been over fifty years and ask how he feels today, he responds, "I'm still waiting to see."

CONCLUSION

*A*s we walk around Ford's former neighborhood, he stops and talks to people that he knows. Ford watched this neighborhood gentrify, but he's much more interested in telling me about where he used to eat breakfast, who worked there, and how much he enjoyed it. I keep bringing up unpleasant things from the past and he keeps telling me something that makes him smile. Sixty years later, Ford is still taking phone calls and networking to solve problems in his community. He explains how each person that we encounter is related to events of the distant past, even if they are the father of someone from a story he likes to tell.

The relationships are clearly important to him, but it feels more like it's the community organizing work that keeps him excited about life. When I ask him if he ever gets tired of all of this, he responds, "They [his community] stepped up to the plate for me, so I do what I can for them." It's true but when I point out that he's an important part of Portland history, he disputes it flatly and immediately. When I suggest that this is modesty, he tells me about someone else who was important in shaping the city. Ford isn't motivated by ego, but merely doing what's moral. I ask him what he's most proud of and he again turns the attention to others, "I'm proud of everyone who came forward to help."

As Martha Gies and Jules Boykoff pointed out in *Oregon Historical Quarterly*, if you reduce the Black Panther story to singular episodes, you miss the broader frame. You have to step away to see that the government carries the responsibility for creating all of these problems in the first place. If you read the Panthers' story in the media, you wouldn't realize that everything they did was about responding to severe structural conditions. Not seeing the bigger picture makes it easy to blame the Panthers and to pick them off, one by one, as Ford initially feared the public would. The Black Panthers' platform was built from frustration and made out of courage and idealism, to recognize what was needed to improve their communities.

The thing that struck me most about the Portland Panthers is their discipline—unlike the police, they didn't have loose cannons among their ranks. They didn't kill anyone or even shoot anyone. While they aimed to radically expose and replace an unjust system, many of their efforts resulted in legislative reform. The thing that makes me chuckle is that the state took a bunch of bookish nerds[87] who were good at campaigning for a seat at the table to solve problems and tried to make them look like a violent, insurrectionist army.

However, when I think about the lengths that the state went to, it ceases to be funny. If you only knew the Portland Black Panther Party from reading the *Oregonian* and *Oregon Journal*, you'd only think of them being associated with criminality. You wouldn't hear about the fact that they are a social services organization. You'd hear about charges being filed against them, but not that the charges were dismissed or dropped.

I ask what happened to the actual hothead firebrand of the story, R.L. Anderson, and Ford tells me that he moved

---

87 To this day, Kent Ford fastidiously revises the two-page reading list that he hands out on his walking tours.

up to Tacoma and became a minister, before a head-on collision took his life. I can't confirm these details because so many people from this era of Portland's history just seem to disappear after 1972. I'm fairly certain that most of them had second acts, but none of them were reported in the media.

In recent years, however, Ford has begun giving more mind to their own legacy. The legacy of the Party as a whole has come into a more favorable light. Fifty years later, glowing articles are appearing in the news. Yet, talking to friends and neighbors, most people don't even know there was a Black Panther Party chapter in Portland, Oregon—let alone all that they accomplished. In 2020, Kent Ford began offering six walking tours per year of historic Black Panther sites in Albina. By 2022, there are several tours per week. I remind Ford that he didn't want to talk to me in 2006. In response, he shares stories of white reporters who told his story from the point of view of the racist police force. "In a world where treachery runs rampant, you don't know who is working for 'the three-letter guys,' or whom you can trust." This makes perfect sense. In our final interview, I asked Ford what motivated this change of heart to speak frequently and publicly about the Black Panthers' legacy and he explained:

> I hung out with a group of young people last Sunday night on Alberta Street. We said, 'Who would have thought that Portland, Oregon would have led the world in racial justice protests?' Things are changing— Ahmaud Arbery's killers were convicted.[88] It's human development—young people are curious about these

88 Ford hesitates here for a minute, reminding me that an all-white jury found him innocent of rioting in 1969—that this progress does go back over fifty years.

things. This week I got invited to talk to a sixth-grade class at Cottonwood School. They want to know the true stories—the treachery of racism and late-stage capitalism. In the beginning, some of the scholars were projecting that it would take about fifty years for change to happen. Now I think it might take one hundred years—longer than for the Palestinians. That doesn't mean we should be inactive. We tried to stay humble and work the street corners and community, without getting big heads. You push when you can and sometimes you pull back and regroup until one day when you win. I tell my story for every comrade who came forward and made the commitment. The new generation of kids, it gives you hope.

Yet, in Portland, hope feels fleeting to many. The previous evening, Ford attended a march protesting yet another police murder. A neighbor left his home, shouting about protesters being "violent terrorists," firing his gun at traffic safety volunteers who tried to de-escalate him, leaving one protester dead and five in critical condition. The shooting made international news and it was revealed that the FBI and the shooter's cousin had warned local police before the incident, who did not act on these reports.[89] As usual, Ford is intimately familiar with the people involved, but he explains that he's seen this enough times that he has ways to cope with it. Events like this are still part of how he sees his role in shaping the future. This is what makes Ford special—even

89 "FBI confirms agents knew of alleged Normandale Park shooter; cousin tried to warn Portland police," OPB, June 16, 2022, opb.org/article/2022/06/16/fbi-confirms-agents-knew-of-alleged-normandale-park-shooter-cousin-tried-to-warn-portland-police/

hours after a horrible tragedy, he doesn't lose hope in the work that he's put in for sixty years of his life.

Seemingly unrelated, at the end of the call, Ford abruptly cuts into a story. "Did I tell you about the time that [future executive editor of the *New York Times*] Bill Keller came up to the Black Panthers' breakfast program? He was in the kitchen and he pointed out a spot to me that needed to be wiped up. I had a rag in my hand. So I handed him the rag and said, 'You clean it.'" In 2014, Keller created the Marshall Project, a nonprofit reporting outfit focused on criminal justice issues in the U.S.

That moment in the kitchen is probably the most powerful story that Ford has ever told me. Regardless of Ford's intent in sharing this story, it evokes how modern activists congratulate themselves for pointing out spots that need to be cleaned up. Whereas Ford's approach—unchanged over sixty years—is not only cleaning up those spots but not letting people stop at pointing to them. Cleaning up the mess remains a shared community effort.

Indeed, to this day, Ford still has the activist spirit and continues to fight for justice. During a recent group tour of Panther historical sites in his old neighborhood, he repeated two mantras: "If they don't come after ya, ya ain't doing nothing right," and "You can save face or your ass, but not both." Ford sees the audience as the next generation of culture change agents but also warned us, "Those three-letter guys, they don't miss a beat!"

It still shocks me that after not speaking for over ten years, I called him out of the blue one day. Despite being a Sunday afternoon and the fact that Ford was attending a BBQ, he answered anyway. I wasn't sure if he remembered me but he was enthusiastically the same activist who saw injustice and reacted, strategically finding a roadmap to achieve his goals. After one long 2021 Saturday together, I asked Ford what advice he has for other people who want to create the world they want to see. As always, he was rather pragmatic, "If you got something that is working, keep working it."

In the middle of a sold-out Black Panther walking tour in July 2022, Kent Ford approached me, beamed, and palmed something small into my hand, in a way that other people couldn't see. I asked "What's this?" and saw that it was a Black Panther Party 55th anniversary button. He wordlessly gave me a half smile in response. I thanked him and placed it in my pocket.

FURTHER READING

Black against Empire: The History and Politics of the Black Panther Party by Joshua Bloom and Waldo E. Martin Jr., University of California (2013)

The Portland Black Panthers: Empowering Albina and Remaking a City by Lucas N. N. Burke and Dr. Judson L. Jeffries, University of Washington (2016)

Body and Soul: The Black Panther Party and the Fight against Medical Discrimination by Alondra Nelson, University of Minnesota (2013)

Black Panther Party: A Graphic Novel History by David F. Walker and Marcus Kwame Anderson, Ten Speed Press (2021)

Behind the Bastards podcast, Robert Evans

Mother Country Radicals podcast, Zayd Ayers Dohrn

The Assassination of Fred Hampton: How the FBI and the Chicago Police Murdered a Black Panther by Jeffrey Haas, Chicago Review Press (2010)

Radicals in the Rose City: Portland's Revolutionaries 1960-1975 by Matt Nelson and Bill Nygren, Northwest History Press (2010)

The Portland Red Guide: Sites & Stories of Our Radical Past, Michael Munk, Ooligan Press (2011)

Pickets, Pistols, and Politics: A History of the Portland Police Association by the Portland Police Bureau, Self-published (1996)

Seize the Time: The Story of the Black Panther Party and Huey P. Newton by Bobby Seale, Black Classic Press (1991)

Revolutionary Suicide by Huey P. Newton, Penguin Classics (1973)

The CIA Makes Science Fiction Unexciting #10: What Happened to the Black Panther Party? by Joseph E. Green, Microcosm Publishing (2019)

Edible Secrets: A Food Tour of Classified U.S. History by Michael Hoerger, Mia Partlow, and Nate Powell, Microcosm Publishing (2010)

Bully. Coward. Victim: The Story of Roy Cohn, Ivy Meeropol, HBO (2020)

"Vortex 1: How a Rock Festival Saved Portland from Chaos" Oregon Public Broadcasting, 2020

Aftermass: How Portland Became North America's #1 Cycling Mecca by Joe Biel, Jeff Hayes, Alice Isley, and Rev Phil Sano, Microcosm Publishing (2014)

Bicycle Culture Rising #2: The Portland Police's Peculiar War Against Bicycling 1993-2007 by Joe Biel, Microcosm Publishing (2010)

White Riot / Black Massacre: A Brief History of the 1921 Tulsa Race Massacre by Kris Rose, Microcosm Publishing (2020)

Robert Smalls: The Slave Who Stole a Confederate Ship, Broke the Code, & Freed a Village by Joe Biel, Microcosm Publishing (2021)

How to Boycott: Make Your Voice Heard, Understand History, & Change the World by Joe Biel, Microcosm Publishing (2019)

Nosedive: History of Albina Gentrification Living in Doomtown by Alec Dunn, Self-published (1997)

Groundswell video series: https://vimeo.com/manage/showcases/4207661/info

The CIA Makes Science Fiction Unexciting: Dark Deeds & Derring-Do by Joe Biel, Microcosm Publishing (2013)

Black Panthers for Beginners by Herb Boyd and Lance Tooks, Camas Books (2018)

The Black Panthers: Portraits from an Unfinished Revolution by Bryan Shih, Yohuru Williams, and Peniel E. Joseph, PublicAffairs (2016)

Up Against the Wall: Violence in the Making and Unmaking of the Black Panther Party by Curtis J. Austin, University of Arkansas Press (2008).

Police Surveillance Photo of Sandra Britt Ford picketing McDonald's, August 1970
Courtesy of Portland City Archives, A2004-005.5319

Police Surveillance Photo of Percy Hampton picketing McDonald's
Courtesy of Portland City Archives, A2004-005.01808